ON LIVING AND DYING

J. Krishnamurti

MORNING LIGHT
PRESS

MORNING LIGHT PRESS

This edition published by
Morning Light Press 2005.

First edition printed 1992
Copyright © 1971 Krishnamurti Foundation Trust Ltd.
Series Editor: Mary Cadogan
Associate Editors: Ray McCoy and David Skitt

Morning Light Press
323 North First, Suite 203
Sandpoint, ID   83864
www.morninglightpress.com
info@mlpress.com

Printed on acid-free paper in Canada.

ISBN: 1-59675-003-0
Philosophy
SAN: 255-3252

Library of Congress Cataloging-in-Publication Data

Krishnamurti, J. (Jiddu), 1895-1986
On living and dying / Jiddu Krishnamurti.-- 2nd ed.
p. cm.
ISBN 1-59675-003-0
1. Life. 2. Death. I. Title.
B5134.K753O564 2005
128--dc22
2005001772

Contents

Foreword

Jiddu Krishnamurti was born in India in 1895 and, at the age of thirteen, taken up by the Theosophical Society, which considered him to be the vehicle for the "world teacher" whose advent it had been proclaiming. Krishnamurti was soon to emerge as a powerful, uncompromising, and unclassifiable teacher, whose talks and writings were not linked to any specific religion and were of neither the East nor the West but for the whole world. Firmly repudiating the messianic image, in 1929 he dramatically dissolved the large and monied organization that had been built around him and declared truth to be "a pathless land," which could not be approached by any formalized religion, philosophy, or sect.

For the rest of his life Krishnamurti insistently rejected the guru status that others tried to foist upon him. He continued to attract large audiences throughout the world but claimed no authority, wanted no disciples, and spoke always as one individual to another. At the core of his teaching was the realization that fundamental changes in society can be brought about only by a transformation of individual consciousness. The need for self-knowledge and understanding of the restrictive, separative influences of religious and nationalistic conditionings was constantly stressed. Krishnamurti pointed always to the urgent need for openness, for the "vast space in the brain in which there is unimaginable energy." This seems to have been the wellspring of his own creativity and the key to his catalytic impact on such a wide variety of people.

Krishnamurti continued to speak all over the world until he died in 1986 at the age of ninety. His talks and dialogues, journals and letters have been collected into more than sixty books. From that vast body of teachings this series of theme books has been compiled. Each book focuses on an issue that has particular relevance to and urgency in our daily lives.

Saanen

I would like to talk about something that includes the totality of life, something that is not fragmentary but a total approach to the whole existence of man. To go into it rather deeply, it seems to me that one must cease to be caught in theories, beliefs, dogmas. Most of us plow incessantly the soil of the mind, but we never seem to sow. We analyze, discuss, tear things to pieces, but we do not understand the whole movement of life.

Now I think there are three things that we have to understand very deeply if we are to comprehend the whole movement of life. They are time, sorrow, and death. To understand time, to comprehend the full significance of sorrow, and to abide with death—all this demands the clarity of love. Love is not a theory, nor is it an ideal. Either you love, or you do not love. It cannot be taught. You cannot take lessons in how to love, nor is there a method by the daily practice of which you can come to know what love is. But I think one comes to love naturally, easily, spontaneously, when one really understands the meaning of time, the extraordinary depth of sorrow, and the purity that comes with death. So perhaps we can consider—factually, not theoretically or abstractly—the nature of time, the quality or structure of sorrow, and the extraordinary thing that we call death. These three things are not separate. If we understand time, we shall understand what death is, and we shall understand also what is sorrow. But if we regard time as something apart from sorrow and death, and try to deal with it separately, then our approach will be fragmentary, and therefore we shall never comprehend the extraordinary beauty and vitality of love.

We are going to deal with time, not as an abstraction but as an actuality—time being duration, the continuity of existence. There is chronological time, hours and days extending into millions of years; and it is chronological time that has produced the mind with which we function. The mind is a result of time as the continuity of existence, and the perfecting or polishing of the mind through that continuity is called progress. Time is also the psychological duration that thought has created as a means of achievement. We use time to progress, to achieve, to become, to bring about a certain result. For most of us, time is a stepping-stone to something far greater—to the development of certain faculties, to the perfecting of a particular technique, to the achievement of an end, a goal, whether praiseworthy or not; so we have come to think that time is necessary to realize what is true, what is God, what is beyond all the travail of man.

Most of us regard time as the period of duration between the present moment and some moment in the future, and we use that time to cultivate character, to get rid of a certain habit, to develop a muscle or an outlook. For two thousand years the Christian mind has been conditioned to believe in a Savior, in hell, in heaven; and in the East a similar conditioning of the mind has been produced over a far longer period. We think that time is necessary for everything that we have to do or understand. Therefore time becomes a burden; it becomes a barrier to actual perception; it prevents us from seeing the truth of something immediately because we think that we must take time over it. We say, "Tomorrow, or in a couple of years, I shall comprehend this thing with extraordinary clarity." The moment we admit time we are cultivating indolence, that peculiar laziness that prevents us from seeing immediately the thing as it actually is.

We think we need time to break through the conditioning that society—with its organized religions, its codes of morality, its dogmas, its arrogance, and its competitive spirit—has imposed upon the mind. We think in terms of time because thought is of time. Thought is the response of memory—memory being the background that has been accumulated, inherited, acquired by the race, by the community, by the group, by the family, and by the individual. This background is the outcome of the additive process of the mind, and its accumulation has taken time. For most of us the mind is memory, and whenever there is a challenge, a demand, it is memory that responds. It is like the response of the electronic brain, which functions through association. Thought being the response of memory, it is in its very nature the product of time and the creator of time.

Please, what I am saying is not a theory; it is not something that you have to think about. You don't have to think about it but rather have to see it, because it is so. I am not going into all the intricate details, but I have indicated the essential facts, and either you see them, or you don't see them. If you are following what is being said, not just verbally, linguistically, or analytically, but if you actually see it is so, you will realize how time deceives. And then the question is whether time can stop. If we are able to see the whole process of our own activity—see its depth, its shallowness, its beauty, its ugliness—not tomorrow, but immediately, then that very perception is the action that destroys time.

Without understanding time, we cannot understand sorrow. They are not two different things as we try to make out. Going to the office, being with one's family, having children—these are not separate, isolated incidents. On the contrary, they are all profoundly and intimately related to each other, and we cannot see this extraordinary intimacy of relationship if there is not the sensitivity that love brings.

To understand sorrow we have really to understand the nature of time and the structure of thought. Time must come to a stop; otherwise, we are merely repeating the information we have accumulated, like an electronic brain. Unless there is an end to time—which means an end to thought—there is mere repetition, adjustment, a continual modification. There is never anything new. We are glorified electronic brains—a bit more independent, perhaps, but still machine-like in the way we function.

To understand the nature of sorrow and the ending of sorrow, one must understand time, and to understand time is to understand thought. The two are not separate. In understanding time, one comes upon thought; and the understanding of thought is the ending of time, and therefore the endings of sorrow. If that is very clear, then we can look at sorrow and not worship it as the Christians do. What we don't understand, we either worship or destroy. We put it in a church, in a temple, or in a dark corner of the mind, and we hold it in awe; or we kick it, throw it away; or we escape from it. But here we are not doing any of those things. We see that for millennia man has struggled with this problem of sorrow, and that he has not been able to resolve it; so he has become hardened to it, he has accepted it, saying it is an inevitable part of life.

Merely to accept sorrow not only is stupid but also makes for a dull mind. It makes the mind insensitive, brutal, superficial, and therefore life becomes very shoddy, a process of mere work and pleasure. One lives a fragmented existence as a businessman, a scientist, an artist, a sentimentalist, a so-called religious person, and so on. But to understand and be free of sorrow, you have to understand time and thereby understand thought. You cannot deny sorrow, or run away, escape from it through entertainment, through churches, through organized beliefs; nor can you accept and worship it; and not to do any of these things demands a great deal of attention, which is energy.

Sorrow is rooted in self-pity, and to understand sorrow there must first be a ruthless operation on all self-pity. I do not know if you have observed how sorry for yourself you become, for example, when you say, "I am lonely." The moment there is self-pity you have provided the soil in which sorrow takes root. However much you may justify your self-pity, rationalize it, polish it, cover it up with ideas, it is still there, festering deep within you. So a man who would understand sorrow must begin by being free of this brutal, self-centered, egotistic triviality that is self-pity. You may feel self-pity because you have a disease, or because you have lost someone by death, or because you have not fulfilled yourself and are therefore frustrated, dull; but whatever its cause, self-pity is the root of sorrow. And when once you are free of self-pity, you can look at sorrow without either worshipping it, or escaping from it, or giving it a sublime, spiritual significance, such as say-ing that you must suffer to find God—which is utter nonsense. Only the dull, stupid mind puts up with sorrow. So there must be no acceptance of sorrow whatsoever, and no denial of it. When you are free of self-pity, you have deprived sorrow of all the sentimentality, all the emotionalism that springs from self-pity. Then you are able to look at sorrow with complete attention.

I hope you are actually doing this with me as we go along and are not just verbally accepting what is being said. Be aware of your own dull acceptance of sorrow, of your rationalizing, your excuses, your self-pity, your sentimentality, your emotional atti-tude towards sorrow, because all that is a dissipation of energy. To understand sorrow, you must give your whole attention to it, and in that attention there is no place for excuses, for sentiment, for rationalization, no place for any self-pity whatsoever.

I hope I am making myself clear when I talk about giving one's whole attention to sorrow. In that attention there is no effort to resolve or to understand sorrow. One is just looking, observ-ing. Any effort to understand, to rationalize, or to escape from sorrow denies that negative state of complete attention in which this thing called sorrow can be understood.

We are not analyzing, we are not analytically investigating sorrow in order to get rid of it, because that is just another trick of the mind. The mind analyzes sorrow and then imagines it has understood and is free of sorrow—which is nonsense. You may get rid of one particular kind of sorrow, but sorrow will come up again in another form. We are talking about sorrow as a total thing—about sorrow as such—whether it is yours, or mine, or that of any other human being.

To understand sorrow there must be understanding of time and thought. There must be a choiceless awareness of all the escapes, of all the self-pity, of all the verbalizations so that the mind becomes completely quiet in front of something that has to be understood. There is then no division between the observer and the thing observed. It is not that *you*, the observer, the thinker, are in sorrow and are looking at that sorrow, but there is only the *state* of sorrow. That state of undivided sorrow is necessary, because when you look at sorrow as an observer you create conflict, which dulls the mind and dissipates energy, and therefore there is no attention.

When the mind understands the nature of time and thought, when it has rooted out self-pity, sentiment, emotionalism, and all the rest of it, then thought—which has created all this complexity—comes to an end, and there is no time; therefore you are directly and intimately in contact with that thing that you call sorrow. Sorrow is sustained only when there is an escape from sorrow, a desire to run away from it, to resolve it, or to worship it. But when there is nothing of all that because the mind is directly in contact with sorrow, and is therefore completely silent with regard to it, then you will discover for yourself that the mind is not in sorrow at all. The moment one's mind is completely in contact with the face of sorrow, that fact itself resolves all the sorrow-producing qualities of time and thought. Therefore there is the ending of sorrow.

Now how are we to understand this thing that we call death of which we are so frightened? Man has created many devious ways of dealing with death—by worshipping it, denying it, clinging to innumerable beliefs, and so on. But to understand death, surely you must come to it afresh; because you really do not know anything about death, do you? You may have seen people die, and you have observed in yourself or in others the coming of old age with its deterioration. You know there is the ending of physical life by old age, by accident, by disease, by murder or suicide, but you do not know death as you know sex, hunger, cruelty, brutality. You do not actually know what it is to die, and until you do, death has no meaning whatsoever. What you are afraid of is an abstraction, something that you do not know. Not knowing the fullness of death, or what its implications are, the mind is frightened of it—frightened of that thought, not of the fact, which it does not know.

Please go into this with me a little bit. If you died instantly, there would be no time to think about death and be frightened of it. But there is a gap between now and the moment when death will come, and during that interval you have plenty of time to worry, to rationalize. You want to carry over to the next life—if there is a next life—all the anxieties, the desires, the knowledge that you have accumulated, so you invent theories, or you believe in some form of immortality. To you, death is something separate from life. Death is over there, while you are here, occupied with living—driving a car, having sex, feeling hunger, worrying, going to the office, accumulating knowledge, and so on. You don't want to die because you haven't finished writing your book, or you don't yet know how to play the violin very beautifully. So you separate death from life, and you say, "I will understand life now, and presently I will understand death." But the two are *not* separate—and that is the first thing to understand. Life and death are one, they are intimately related, and you cannot isolate one of them and try to understand it apart from the other. But most of us do that. We separate life into unrelated watertight compartments. If you are an economist, then economics is all that you are concerned with, and you don't know anything about the rest. If you are a doctor whose specialty is the nose and throat, or the heart, you live in that limited field of knowledge for forty years, and that is your heaven when you die.

To deal with life fragmentarily is to live in constant confusion, contradiction, misery. You have to see the totality of life, and you can see the totality of it only when there is affection, when there is love. Love is the only revolution that will produce order. It is no good acquiring more and more knowledge about mathematics, about medicine, about history, about economics, and then putting all the fragments together; that will not solve a thing. Without love, revolution leads only to the worship of the State, or to the worship of an image, or to innumerable tyrannical corruptions and the destruction of man. Similarly, when the mind, because it is frightened, puts death at a distance and separates it from daily living, that separation only breeds more fear, more anxiety, and the multiplication of theories about death. To understand death, you have to understand life. But life is not the continuity of thought; it is this very continuity that has bred all our misery.

So can the mind bring death from the distant to the immediate? Do you follow? Actually, death is not somewhere far away; it is here and now. It is here when you are talking, when you are enjoying yourself, when you are listening, when you are going to the office. It is here at every minute of life, just as love is. If once you perceive this fact, then you will find that there is no fear of death at all. One is afraid not of the unknown but of losing the known. You are afraid of losing your family, or being left alone, without companions; you are afraid of the pain of loneliness, of being without the experiences, the possessions that you have gathered. It is the known that we are afraid to let go of. The known is memory, and to that memory the mind clings. But memory is only a mechanical thing—which the computers are demonstrating very beautifully.

To understand the beauty and the extraordinary nature of death, there must be freedom from the known. In dying to the known is the beginning of the understanding of death, because then the mind is made fresh, new, and there is no fear. Therefore one can enter into that state called death. So, from the beginning to the end, life and death are one. The wise man understands time, thought, and sorrow, and only he can understand death. The mind that is dying each minute, never accumulating, never gathering experience, is innocent, and is therefore in a constant state of love.

Ojai

Questioner: You have said that death, love, birth, are essentially one. How can you maintain that there is no distinction between the shock and sorrow of death and the bliss of love?

Krishnamurti: What do you mean by death? Loss of body, loss of memory, and you hope and you think and you believe that there is a continuance afterward. Something gone from here—that is what you call death. Now to me, death is brought about by the continuance of memory, and memory is but the result of craving, grasping, wanting. So to a person who is free from craving, there is no death, neither a beginning nor an end, neither the path of love nor the path of mind, sorrow. Please, I was trying to explain, in the pursuit of an opposite we create a resistance. If I am fearful, I seek courage, yet fear pursues me because I am only escaping from one to the other. Whereas if I free myself from fear, I do not know either courage or fear, and I say the manner of doing that is to become aware, watchful, not to try to grasp courage but to be free of motive in action. That is, if you are fearful, do not create a motive for action of courage but free yourself from fear. That is action without a motive. You will see, if you really have understood this, that time, that death as a future, has ceased. Death is but the awareness of an intense loneliness, and so, being caught up in loneliness, we rush to the other, we want unity, or to find out what exists on the other side, which to me are the pursuits of opposites, and therefore they hold loneliness ever. Whereas, in facing loneliness, rejoicing in it fully, knowing with awareness, you destroy that loneliness in the present. Therefore there is no death.

All things must wear out. Things are bodies, qualities, resistance, hindrances; they all will wear out, must wear out, but the man who is free in thought, and emotions, from that resistance, hindrance, he shall know immortality, not the continuance of his own limitation, of his own personality, individuality, which is but a series of layers of cravings, graspings, wantings. You may disagree, but if you are free of thought, if you have pierced through that self-consciousness, through watchfulness, through that flame of intensity, then there is immortality, which is perfect harmony, which is not "the path of love" or "the path of sorrow" but is that in which all distinction has ceased.

Bombay

Questioner: The fact of death stares everybody in the face, yet its mystery is never solved. Must it always be so?

Krishnamurti: Why is there a fear of death? When we cling to continuity, there is the fear of death. Incomplete action brings the fear of death. There is a fear of death as long as there is the desire for continuity in character, continuity in action, in capacity, in the name, and so on. As long as there is action seeking a result, there must be the thinker who is seeking continuity. Fear comes into being when this continuity is threatened through death. So, there is fear of death as long as there is the desire for continuity.

That which continues disintegrates. Any form of continuity, however noble, is a process of disintegration. In continuity there is never renewal, and only in renewal is there freedom from the fear of death. If we see the truth of this, then we will see the truth in the false. Then there would be the liberation from the false. Then there would be no fear of death. Thus living, experiencing, is in the present and not a means of continuity.

Is it possible to live from moment to moment with renewal? There is renewal only in ending and not in continuity. In the interval between the ending and the beginning of another problem, there is renewal.

Death, the state of non-continuity, the state of rebirth, is the unknown. Death is the unknown. The mind, which is the result of continuity, cannot know the unknown. It can know only the known. It can only act and have its being in the known, which is continuous. So the known is in fear of the unknown. The known can never know the unknown, and so death remains the mystery. If there is an ending from moment to moment, from day to day, in this ending the unknown comes into being.

Immortality is not the continuation of "me." The me and the mine is of time, the result of action towards an end. So there is no relationship between the me and the mine and that which is immortal, timeless. We would like to think there is a relationship, but this is an illusion. That which is immortal cannot be encased in that which is mortal. That which is immeasurable cannot be caught in the net of time.

There is fear of death where there is search for fulfillment. Fulfillment has no ending. Desire is constantly seeking and changing the object of fulfillment, and so it is caught in the net of time. So the search for self-fulfillment is another form of continuity, and frustration seeks death as a means of continuity. Truth is not continuous. Truth is a state of being, and being is action without time. This being can be experienced only when desire, which gives birth to continuity, is wholly and completely understood. Thought is founded on the past, so thought cannot know the unknown, the immeasurable. The thought process must come to an end. Then only the unknowable comes into being.

Varanasi

Questioner: I am afraid of death. What is death, and how can I cease to be afraid of it?

Krishnamurti: It is very easy to ask a question. There is no "yes" or "no" answer to life. But our minds demand "yes" or "no" because they have been trained in what to think and not in how to understand, how to see things. When we say, "What is death, and how can I not be afraid of it?" we want formulas, we want definitions, but we never know how to think about the problem.

Let us see if we can think out the problem together. What is death? Ceasing to be, is it not, coming to an end? We know that there is an ending; we see that every day all around us. But I do not want to die, the "I" being the process: "I am thinking, I am experiencing, my knowledge," the things that I have cultivated, the things against which I have resisted, the character, the experience, the knowledge, the precision, and the capacity, the beauty. I do not want all that to end. I want to go on; I have not yet finished; I do not want to come to an end. Yet there is an ending. Obviously every organism that is functioning must come to an end. But my mind won't accept that. So, I begin to invent a creed, a continuity; I want to accept this because I have complete theories, complete conditioning that I continue, that there is reincarnation.

We are not disputing whether or not there is continuity, whether or not there is rebirth. That is not the problem. The problem is that even though you have such beliefs, you are still afraid. Because, after all, there is no certainty; there is always uncertainty. There is always this hankering after an assurance. So the mind, knowing the ending, begins to have fear, longs to live as long as possible, seeks for more and more palliatives. The mind also believes in continuity after death.

What is continuity? Does not continuity imply time, not the mere chronological time by a watch but time as a psychological process? I want to live. Because I think it is a continued process without any ending, my mind is always adding, gathering to itself in the hope of continuity. So the mind thinks in terms of time, and if it can have continuity in time, then it is not afraid.

What is immortality? The continuity of the "me" is what we call immortality—the "me" at a higher level. You hope that the me will continue. The me is still within the field of thought, is it not? You have thought about it. The me, however superior you may think it to be, is the product of thought; and that is conditioned, is born of time. Please, do not merely follow the logic of what I say but see the full significance of it. Really, immortality is not of time and therefore not of the mind, not a thing born out of my longings, my demands, my fears, my urges.

One sees that life has an ending, a sudden ending. What lived yesterday may not live today, and what lives today may not live tomorrow. Life certainly has an ending. It is a fact, but we won't admit it. You are different from yesterday. Various things, various contacts, reactions, compulsions, resistances, influences, change "what was," or put an end to it. A man who is really creative must have an ending, and he accepts it. But we won't accept it because our minds are so accustomed to the process of accumulation. We say, "I have learned this today," "I learned that yesterday." We think only in terms of time, in terms of continuity. If we do not think in terms of continuity, there will be an ending, there will be dying, and we will see things clearly, as simple as they are, directly.

We do not admit the fact of ending because our minds seek, in continuity, security in the family, in property, in our profession, in any job we do. Therefore we are afraid. It is only a mind that is free from the acquisitive pursuit of security, free from the desire to continue, from the process of continuity, that will know what immortality is. But the mind that is seeking personal immortality, the me wanting to continue, will never know what mortality is; such a mind will never know the significance of fear and death, and go beyond.

With Students at Rajghat

Questioner: *Why do we fear death?*

Krishnamurti: You have asked the question: "Why do we fear death?" Do you know what death is? You see the green leaf; it has lived all the summer, danced in the wind, absorbed the sunlight; the rains have washed it clean; and when the winter comes, the leaf withers and dies. The bird on the wing is a beautiful thing, and it too withers and dies. You see human bodies being carried to the river to be burned. So you know what death is. Why are you afraid of it? Because you are living like the leaf, like the bird, and a disease or something else happens to you, and you are finished. So you say, "I want to live, I want to enjoy, I want to have this thing called life go on in me." So the fear of death is the fear of coming to an end, is it not? Playing cricket, enjoying the sunlight, seeing the river again, putting on your old clothes, reading books, meeting your friends constantly—all that comes to an end. So you are frightened of death.

Being frightened of death, knowing that death is inevitable, we think of how to go beyond death; we have various theories. But if we know how to end, there is no fear; if we know how to die each day, then there is no fear. You understand this? It is a little bit out of the line. We do not know how to die because we are always gathering, gathering, gathering. We always think in terms of tomorrow: "I am this, and I will be that." We are never complete in a day; we do not live as though there is only one day to be lived. You understand what I am talking about? We are always living in the tomorrow or in the yesterday. If somebody told you that you were going to die at the end of the day, what would you do? Would you not live richly for that day? We do not live the rich fullness of a day. We do not worship the day; we are always thinking of what we will be tomorrow, of the cricket game that we are going to finish tomorrow, of the examination that we are going to finish in six months, of how we are going to enjoy our food, of what kind of clothes we are going to buy, and so on, always tomorrow or yesterday. And so we are never living; we are always really dying in the wrong sense.

If we live one day and finish with it and begin again another day as if it were something new, fresh, then there is no fear of death. To die each day to all the things that we have acquired, to all knowledge, to all the memories, to all the struggles, not to carry them over to the next day—in that there is beauty; even though there is an ending, there is a renewal.

The Fear of Death

On the red earth in front of the house there were quantities of trumpet-like flowers with golden hearts. They had large, mauve petals and a delicate scent. They would be swept away during the day, but in the darkness of night they covered the red earth. The creeper was strong with serrated leaves that glistened in the morning sun. Some children carelessly trod on the flowers, and a man getting hurriedly into his car never even looked at them. A passerby picked one, smelled it, and carried it away, to be dropped presently. A woman who must have been a servant came out of the house, picked a flower, and put it in her hair. How beautiful those flowers were, and how quickly they were withering in the sun!

Questioner: I have always been haunted by some kind of fear. As a child I was very timid, shy, and sensitive, and now I am afraid of old age and death. I know we must all die, but no amount of rationalizing seems to calm this fear. I have joined the Psychical Research Society, attended a few séances, and read what the great teachers have said about death; but fear of it is still there. I even tried psychoanalysis, but that was no good either. This fear has become quite a problem to me; I wake up in the middle of the night with frightful dreams, and all of them are in one way or another concerned with death. I am strangely frightened of violence and death. The war was a continual nightmare to me, and now I am really very disturbed. It is not a neurosis, but I can see that it might become one. I have done everything that I possibly can to control this fear; I have tried to run away from it, but at the end of my escape I have not been able to shake it off. I have listened to a few rather stupid lectures on reincarnation, and have somewhat studied the Hindu and Buddhist literature concerning it. But all this has been very unsatisfactory, at least to me. I am not just superficially afraid of death, but there is a very deep fear of it.

Krishnamurti: How do you approach the future, the tomorrow, death? Are you trying to find the truth of the matter, or are you seeking reassurance, a gratifying assertion of continuity or annihilation? Do you want the truth or a comforting answer?

Questioner: *When you put it that way, I really do not know what I am afraid of, but the fear is both there and urgent.*

Krishnamurti: What is your problem? Do you want to be free from fear, or are you seeing the truth regarding death?

Questioner: *What do you mean by the truth regarding death?*

Krishnamurti: Death is an unavoidable fact; do what you will, it is irrevocable, final, and true. But do you want to know the truth of what is beyond death?

Questioner: *Everything I have studied and the few materializations I have seen at séances make it obvious that there is some kind of continuity after death. Thought in some form continues, which you yourself have asserted. Just as the broadcasting of songs, words, and pictures requires a receiver at the other end, so thought that continues after death needs an instrument through which it* *can express itself. The instrument may be a medium, or thought may incarnate itself in another manner. This is all fairly clear and can be experimented with and understood; but even though I have gone into this matter fairly deeply, there is still an unfathomable fear that I think is definitely connected with death.*

Krishnamurti: Death is inevitable. Continuity can be ended, or it can be nourished and maintained. That which has continuity can never renew itself. It can never be the new; it can never understand the unknown. Continuity is duration, and that which is everlasting is not the timeless. Through time, duration, the timeless is not. There must be ending for the new to be. The new is not within the continuation of thought. Thought is continuous movement in time; this movement cannot enclose within itself a state of being that is not of time. Thought is founded on the past; its very being is of time. Time is not only chronological but it is also thought as a movement of the past through the present to the future; it is the movement of memory, of the word, the picture, the symbol, the record, the repetition. Thought, memory, is continuous through word and repetition. The ending of thought is the beginning of the new; the death of thought is life eternal. There must be constant ending for the new to be. That which is new is not continuous; the new can never be within the field of time. The new is only in death from moment to moment. There must be death every day for the unknown to be. The ending is the beginning, but fear prevents the ending.

Questioner: *I know I have fear, and I don't know what is beyond it.*

Krishnamurti: What do we mean by fear? What is fear? Fear is not an abstraction; it does not exist independently, in isolation. It comes into being only in relation to something. In the process of relationship fear manifests itself; there is no fear apart from relationship. Now what is it that you are afraid of? You said you are afraid of death. What do we mean by death? Though we have theories, speculations, and there are certain observable facts, death is still the unknown. Whatever we may know about it, death itself cannot be brought into the field of the known; we stretch out a hand to grasp it, but it is not. Association is the known, and the unknown cannot be made familiar; habit cannot capture it, so there is fear.

Can the known, the mind, ever comprehend or contain the unknown? The hand that stretches out can receive only the knowable; it cannot hold the unknowable. To desire experience is to give continuity to thought; to desire experience is to give strength to the past; to desire experience is to further the known. You want to experience death, do you not? Though living, you want to know what death is. But do you know what living is? You know life only as conflict, confusion, antagonism, passing joy and pain. But is that life? Are struggle and sorrow life? In this state that we call life we want to experience something that is not in our own field of consciousness. This pain, this struggle, the hate that is enfolded in joy, is what we call living; and we want to experience something that is the opposite of what we call living. The opposite is the continuation of what is, perhaps modified. But death is not the opposite. It is the unknown. The knowable craves to experience death, the unknown; but, do what it will, it cannot experience death. Therefore it is fearful; is that it?

Questioner: *You have stated it clearly. If I could know or experience what death is while living, then surely fear would cease.*

Krishnamurti: Because you cannot experience death, you are afraid of it. Can the conscious experience that state that is not to be brought into being through the conscious? That which can be experienced is the projection of the conscious, the known. The known can only experience the known; experience is always within the field of the known; the known cannot experience what is beyond its field. Experiencing is utterly different from experience. Experiencing is not within the field of the experiencer. But as experiencing fades, the experiencer and the experience come into being, and then experiencing is brought into the field of the known. The knower, the experiencer, craves for the state of experiencing the unknown; and as the experiencer, the knower, cannot enter into the state of experiencing, he is afraid. He *is* fear; he is not separate from it. The experiencer of fear is not an observer of it; he *is* fear itself, the very instrument of fear.

Questioner: What do you mean by fear? I know I am afraid of death. I don't feel that I am fear, but I am fearful of something. I fear and am separate from fear. Fear is a sensation distinct from the "I" who is looking at it, analyzing it. I am the observer, and fear is the observed. How can the observer and the observed be one?

Krishnamurti: You say that you are the observer and fear is the observed. But is that so? Are you an entity separate from your qualities? Are you not identical with your qualities? Are you not your thoughts, emotions, and so on? You are not separate from your qualities, thoughts. You *are* your thoughts. Thought creates the "you," the supposedly separate entity; without thought, the thinker is not. Seeing the impermanence of itself, thought creates the thinker as the permanent, the enduring; and the thinker then becomes the experiencer, the analyzer, the observer separate from the transient. We all crave some kind of permanence, and seeing impermanence about us, thought creates the thinker, who is supposed to be permanent. The thinker then proceeds to build up other and higher states of permanency: the soul, the atman, the higher self, and so on. Thought is the foundation of this whole structure. But that is another matter. We are concerned with fear. What is fear? Let us see what it is.

You say you are afraid of death. Since you cannot experience it, you are afraid of it. Death is the unknown, and you are afraid of the unknown. Is that it? Now, can you be afraid of that which you do not know? If something is unknown to you, how can you be afraid of it? You are really afraid not of the unknown, of death, but of loss of the known, because that might cause pain, or take away your pleasure, your gratification. It is the known that causes fear, not the unknown. How can the unknown cause fear? It is not measurable in terms of pleasure and pain: it is unknown.

Fear cannot exist by itself; it comes in relationship to something. You are actually afraid of the known in its relation to death, are you not? Because you cling to the known, to an experience, you are frightened of what the future might be. But the "what might be," the future, is merely a reaction, a speculation, the opposite of what *is*. This is so, is it not?

Questioner: *Yes, that seems to be right.*

Krishnamurti: And do you know what *is*? Do you understand it? Have you opened the cupboard of the known and looked into it? Are you not also frightened of what you might discover there? Have you ever inquired into the known, into what you possess?

Questioner: *No, I have not. I have always taken the known for granted. I have accepted the past as one accepts sunlight or rain. I have never considered it; one is almost unconscious of it, as one is of one's shadow. Now that you mention it, I suppose I am also afraid to find out what might be there.*

Krishnamurti: Are not most of us afraid to look at ourselves? We might discover unpleasant things, so we would rather not look. We prefer to be ignorant of what is. We are afraid not only of what might be in the future but also of what might be in the present. We are afraid to know ourselves as we are, and this avoidance of what is is making us afraid of what might be. We approach the so-called known with fear, and also the unknown, death. The avoidance of what is is the desire for gratification. We are seeking security, constantly demanding that there shall be no disturbance, and it is this desire not to be disturbed that makes us avoid what is and fear what might be. Fear is the ignorance of what is, and our life is spent in a constant state of fear.

Questioner: But how is one to get rid of this fear?

Krishnamurti: To get rid of something, you must understand it. Is there fear, or only the desire not to see? It is the desire not to see that brings on fear; and when you don't want to understand the full significance of what is, fear acts as a preventive. You can lead a gratifying life by deliberately avoiding all inquiry into what is, and many do this; but they are not happy, nor are those who amuse themselves with a superficial study of what is. Only those who are earnest in their inquiry can be aware of happiness; to them alone is there freedom from fear.

Questioner: Then how is one to understand what is?

Krishnamurti: The what is is to be seen in the mirror of relationship, relationship with all things. The what is cannot be understood in withdrawal, in isolation; it cannot be understood if there is the interpreter, the translator who denies or accepts. The what is can be understood only when the mind is utterly passive, when it is not operating on what is.

Questioner: *Is it not extremely difficult to be passively aware?*

Krishnamurti: It is, as long as there is thought.

Seattle

Questioner: What is death that one should be afraid of it?

Krishnamurti: Do you know what death is? Are you not afraid of it?

Questioner: Yes.

Questioner: No.

Krishnamurti: You are not afraid of coming to an end? Then you must be very fed up with life! What is death if it is not coming to an end? Are you not afraid of leaving all your memories, your experiences, your loved ones, all that which is you?

Questioner: We do not know death; we only know what someone else's death is.

Krishnamurti: Death, obviously, is something we do not know; we can only experience it indirectly. To die is to come to an end, physically as well psychologically.

Questioner: We are concerned not with the problem of death but with the problem of the fear of death.

Krishnamurti: So let us go into the problem together; let us experience it, explore it together.

We are afraid of death. We are not afraid of something that we definitely and positively know. There is fear only in relation to that which is uncertain, which might hurt us, which makes us insecure. Death is an uncertainty, and that is why we are afraid of it. If we could know the whole content, the whole import of death, know the whole significance of what is beyond, then we would have no fear, would we? So how can we know what it is to die? How can we while living know death?

Questioner: How can we know it without experiencing it?

Krishnamurti: We are going to see in a minute. How difficult it is for us to understand the ways of the mind! The mind wants to make the unknown into the known—and that is one of our difficulties. The mind says, "If I do not know what is beyond death, I am afraid; but if you can assure me that there is a continuity, then I cease to be afraid." The mind is seeking certainty; but as long as we are seeking certainty, there must be fear. It is not of death that we are afraid but of being uncertain. We can function only when we have a feeling of security, and if that is taken away from us, we get frightened. So if we can find out what death is, then we shall be free of fear.

Questioner: If I think of death as an end, how can I have a feeling of security as long as I want to continue? On the other hand, how can I be rid of my desire for certainty?

Krishnamurti: One can be rid of it only when one is aware that there is no certainty.

Questioner: But we want to be certain of the future.

Krishnamurti: Can we be? We want to be sure that we have lived in the past and that we will have a continuity in the future. We can read all that the religious books say; we can listen to other people's experiences and seek the assurance of mediums; but will that make us free from fear? As long as we are seeking certainty, we must be afraid of uncertainty. Please, this is not a conundrum. The search for the opposite, for the antithesis of what we are, the desire to avoid, to run away from what we are, creates fear, does it not? So we must obviously understand what fear is. What is fear?

There is the fact of death, and we say that we are afraid of that fact. Does fear come into being because of the fact, or because of the word *death*, or is the sensation independent of the word? We respond to words. Words like *God, love, communism*, and *democracy* create in us definite nervous and psychological responses, do they not? When we believe in "God" and talk about "Him," we feel better. Words like *death, hate, Germans, Russians, Hindus*, and *Negroes* all have an extraordinarily deep significance for us. Therefore we must find out whether that sensation that we call fear is an actuality, or whether it is merely the result of the words we use.

Questioner: The actuality is the meaning we give to the word.

Krishnamurti: Let us go into it. If we earnestly want to be free from fear, we must find out what is the right approach to it. We can see various factors that make us afraid of this thing called death, but I wonder whether there is not still another cause, whether the very word *death* is not responsible for our fear because of its meaning, the associations it evokes in our minds. Please follow this, and we will see what comes out of it. The word *death* is not death itself, yet it has great significance for us, has it not?

Questioner: *The word carries a connotation of finality.*

Krishnamurti: Yes, and also of all the fears of the race, of the class, of the individual. Our minds have been conditioned, not only by that word, but by words such as *capitalism, fascism, peace, war,* and many others. Is that not so? Words, symbols, images have a great deal of importance for us, much more so than facts, because we cannot think without words. The word is the image, the symbol, and our thinking is verbalizing, symbolizing, imagining, labeling. If we had not images, symbols, or words, we would have no memory, would we? So, it is not the *fact* of death but the word *death* that gives us the feeling of fear. No? We also see that fear arises when the mind, which is accustomed to certainty, is confronted with uncertainty; when the mind, which is the result of the known, the past, confronts the unknown, the future.

Now the next question is this: Would the sensation that we call fear be there if we did not give it the name "fear"? Would the sensation exist without the word?

Questioner: *The word is just a label for the sensation. We have to give a name to the sensation; it is our only way of recognizing it.*

Krishnamurti: When we consider the fear of death, does the sensation or the word come first? Does the word bring on the sensation, or is the sensation independent of the word? This is really quite an important question, for if we can go into it, I think we will see something rather significant.

When we are confronted with the fact of death, we name it, and the name gives us a feeling of uncertainty, which we dislike and which makes us afraid. Now death is something new; the fact of death is a new challenge, is it not? Yet the moment we give it a name, we have rendered it the old. Whenever the mind meets a new fact, a new incident, a new sensation, it immediately labels it, recognizes it, identifies it, for we think that that is the only way we have of understanding anything: to bring the new into the old. That is the way the mind functions, is it not? That is what we do instantaneously. It is probably an unconscious act, but it is our immediate response. The mind cannot think about the new, so it always translates it in terms of the old. Thinking is a process of verbalization, is it not? When we are challenged by the fact that we call death, we respond by thinking about it, and that verbalization creates fear. Now the problem is whether it is possible, when we are challenged by that which we have termed *death*, not to respond verbally.

Questioner: I would say no.

Krishnamurti: If you have not tried it, how can you say "yes" or "no"? When I ask you this question, you are being challenged by something, and your immediate response is to try to find an answer; your mind goes into operation, and at once the words come out. Please watch your own mind, and you will see that when you are asked something that you do not know, the mind does not remain silent and try to understand the new but immediately begins looking in the old records of memory for the right answer.

Questioner: The logical conclusion of your reasoning would be to stop the thinking process.

Krishnamurti: Please, this is not logical reasoning; it is factual observation. You will see what happens if you experience it. When the mind meets something new for which it has no answer, for which there are no words, it becomes quiet. When we see something totally new that we do not recognize and cannot identify with anything we already know, we do not name it. We watch to find out what it is, and there is no verbalizing in that state of watchful attention. The moment we start verbalizing, any experience ceases to be new and becomes the old, does it not?

Questioner: *If it is entirely new, there is nothing to verbalize about.*

Krishnamurti: Surely. So, death is something new if we do not verbalize about it. Though it is a word, the content of that word, its conditioning quality, has gone out of it. Then we can look at death. Now what is the state of the mind that is challenged by the new and does not verbalize about it, does not immediately respond by looking in the old memories, the old records, in order to find the right answer? Is not that mind also new? The old conditionings have fallen away, the agitation has ceased, the search has come to an end. And when the challenge is new, and the mind is new, where is fear?

Questioner: *The mind is new, but the challenge is still the old, even without a name.*

Krishnamurti: Death is the old only when we recognize it, and we can recognize it only through words, through memory, which is one's conditioning. Death is the old because it has all the connotations of fear, belief, consolation, escape. We have always approached it with the known; our approach is the old approach, and so we recognize it as death. But if we have a new approach, if we come to it with a new mind, completely denuded of the old, it may no longer be that which we call death; it may be something entirely different.

Questioner: *We must know what we are looking at, even if we do not give it a name.*

Krishnamurti: That is what I am proposing that we do. Let us try to find out whether it is possible for the mind to stop the process of verbalization and merely look. If the mind can do that, then is this thing that the mind is looking at, and that is the new, separate from the mind itself, which is also the new? Is there a division between the challenge and the observer who looks at the challenge?

Questioner: *The observer creates the challenge.*

Krishnamurti: You are too quick in answering. Please do not translate what I am saying into your own terms, because then you will miss the whole significance of it.

Questioner: *If they are both new, then how can we say that they are either the same or different?*

Krishnamurti: When the mind is new, is the challenge, which is also new, outside of it?

The difficulty with all this is that unless we really experience it, it will have little meaning for us. That which is new has no death, it is continually becoming, it is never the old. It is only the old that is afraid of coming to an end; and if we go into this whole question very, very profoundly, we will see that it is possible for the mind to be free, not only from the fear of death but also from fear in all its forms.

Paris

In considering fear and sorrow, one has to go into this problem of death and old age. Death may happen through disease, through an accident, or through old age and decay. There is the obvious fact of the physical organism coming to an end. And there is also the obvious fact of the organism growing old, becoming old, diseased, and dying. And one observes, as one grows older, the problem it constitutes, its ugliness, how as one grows older one becomes more dull, more insensitive. Old age becomes a problem when one does not know how to live. One may never have lived at all—one has lived in struggle, pain, conflict, which is expressed in our faces, in our bodies, in our attitudes.

As the physical organism comes to an end, death is certainly inevitable. Perhaps the scientists may discover some pill that will give continuity for another fifty or hundred years, but always at the end there is death. There is always the problem of old age, losing one's memory, becoming senile, more and more useless to society, and so on. And there is death, death as something inevitable, unknown, most unpleasant, most dreaded. Being frightened of it, we never even talk about it, or if we do talk about it, we have theories, comforting formulas, either the "reincarnation" of the East or the "resurrection" of the West. Or perhaps intellectually we accept death and say it is inevitable and that "as everything dies, I will also die." Rationalization, a comforting belief, and an escape are all exactly the same.

But what is death? Apart from the physical entity coming to an end, what is death? In asking that question, one must ask what is living? The two cannot be separated. If you say, "I really want to know what death is," you will never know the answer unless you know what living is. And what is our living? From the moment we are born until we die, it consists of endless struggle, a battlefield, not only within ourselves but also with our neighbors, with our wife, children, with our husband, with everything—it is a battle of sorrow, fear, anxiety, guilt, loneliness, and despair. And out of this despair come the inventions of the mind such as gods, saviors, saints, the worship of heroes, rituals, and war—actual war, killing each other. That's our life. That's what we call living, in which there may be a moment of joy, an occasional light in the eye, but that's our life. And to that life we cling because we say, "At least I know that, and it is better to have that than nothing."

So one is afraid of living, and one is afraid of death, the ending. And when death comes inevitably, one fights it off. Our life is one long-drawn-out agony of battle with ourselves, with everything about us. And this battle is what is called love; it is a mounting pleasure, a mounting desire, with its fulfillment, sexually or otherwise—all that is our life from morning until night.

Unless one understands living, merely to find a way out of death is utterly meaningless. When one understands what it is to live, which is to end sorrow, to end struggle, not to make a battlefield of life, then it will be seen psychologically, inwardly, that to live is to die—to die to everything every day, to all the accumulations that have been gathered, so that the mind is fresh, new, and innocent each day. And that requires enormous attention. But this cannot be unless there is an ending to sorrow, that is, fear, and so the ending of thought. Then the mind is completely quiet—not dull, not stupid, not made insensitive by discipline and all the rest of those tricks that one plays through the study of yoga and all the rest of that business. Then life is dying, which means there is no death without love. Love is not a memory. Life, love, and death go together; they are not separate things. And so life consists in living every day in a state of freshness; and to have that clarity, that innocence, there must be the death of that state of mind in which there is always the center, the "me." Without love there is no virtue. Without love there is no peace; there is no relationship. That is the foundation for the mind to go immeasurably into that dimension in which alone truth exists.

Amsterdam

We have to understand another phenomenon of life, which is death: death from old age, or disease, and accidental death, through disease, or naturally. We grow old inevitably, and that age is shown in the way we have lived our life, it shows in our face, whether we have satisfied our appetites crudely, brutally. We lose sensitivity, the sensitivity we had when young, fresh, innocent. And as we grow older we become insensitive, dull, unaware, and gradually enter the grave.

So there is old age. And there is this extraordinary thing called death, of which most of us are dreadfully frightened. If we are not frightened, we have rationalized this phenomenon intellectually and have accepted the edicts of the intellect. But it is still there. And obviously there is the ending of the organism, the body. And we accept that naturally, because we see everything dying. But what we do not accept is the psychological ending, of the "me," with the family, with the house, with success, the things I have done, and the things I have still to do, the fulfillments and the frustrations—and there is something more to do before I end! And the psychological entity, we're afraid that will come to an end—the "me," the "I," the "soul," in the various forms, words, that we give to the center of our being.

Does it come to an end? Does it have a continuity? The East has said it has a continuity: there is reincarnation, being born better in the next life if you have lived rightly. If you believe in reincarnation, as the whole of Asia does (I don't know why they do, but if gives them a great deal of comfort), then in that idea is implied, if you observe it very closely, that what you do now, every day, matters tremendously. Because in the next life you're going to pay for it or be rewarded depending on how you have lived. So what matters is not what you believe will happen in the next life but what you are and how you live. And that is implied also when you talk about resurrection. *Here* (in the West) you have symbolized it in one person and worship that person, because you yourself don't know how to be reborn again in your life *now* (not "in heaven at the right hand of God," whatever that may mean).

So what matters is how you live *now*—not what your beliefs are—but what you are, what you do. But we are afraid that the center, called the "I," may come to an end. We ask: Does it come to an end? Please listen to this!

You have lived in thought; that is, you have given tremendous importance to thinking. But thinking is old; thinking is never new; thinking is the continuation of memory. If you have lived there, obviously there is some kind of continuity. And it is a continuity that is dead, over, finished. It is something old; only that which ends can have something new. So dying is very important to understand; to die; to die to everything that one knows. I don't know if you have ever tried it. To be free from the known, to be free from your memory, even for a few days, to be free from your pleasure, without any argument, without any fear, to die to your family, to your house, to your name, to become completely anonymous. It is only the person who is completely anonymous who is in a state of non-violence, who has no violence. And so to die every day, not as an idea but actually—*do* do it sometime!

You know, one has collected so much, not only books, houses, the bank account, but inwardly, the memories of insults, the memories of flattery, the memories of neurotic achievements, the memory of holding on to your own particular experience, which gives you a position. To die to all that without argument, without discussion, without any fear, just to give it up. Do it sometime, you'll see. It used to be the tradition in the East that a rich man every five years or so gave up everything, including his money, and began again. You can't do that nowadays; there are too many people, everyone wanting your job, the population explosion, and all the rest of it. But to do it psychologically—not giving up your wife, your clothes, your husband, your children, or your house, but inwardly—is not to be attached to anything. In that there is great beauty. After all, it is love, isn't it? Love is not attachment. When there is attachment, there is fear. And fear inevitably becomes authoritarian, possessive, oppressive, dominating.

So meditation is the understanding of life, which is to bring about order. Order is virtue, which is light. This light is not to be lit by another, however experienced, however clever, however erudite, however spiritual. Nobody on earth or in heaven can light that except yourself in your own understanding and meditation.

To die to everything within oneself! For love is innocent and fresh, young, and clear. Then, if you have established this order, this virtue, this beauty, this light in yourself, then you can go beyond. This means that the mind, having laid order— which is not of thought—the mind then becomes utterly quiet, silent, naturally, without any force, without any discipline. And in the light of that silence all actions can take place, the daily living, from that silence. And if one were lucky enough to have gone that far, then in that silence there is quite a different movement, which is not of time, which is not of words, which is not measurable by thought, because it is always new. It is that immeasurable something that man has everlastingly sought. But you have to come upon it; it cannot be given to you. It is not the word or the symbol; those are destructive. But for it to come, you must have complete order, beauty, love. Therefore you must die to everything that you know psychologically, so that your mind is clear, not tortured, so that it sees things as they are, both outwardly and inwardly.

From *The Flight of the Eagle*
London, 20 March 1969

Fragmentation

What is death? What is the relationship between love and death? I think we will find the relationship between the two when we understand the meaning of death. To understand that we must obviously understand what living is. What actually is our living—the daily living, not the ideological, the intellectual something, which we consider should be, but which is really false? What actually is our daily living of conflict, despair, loneliness, isolation? Our life is a battlefield, sleeping and waking. We try to escape from this in various ways: through music, art, museums, religious or philosophical entertainment, spinning a lot of theories, being caught up in knowledge, anything but putting an end to this conflict, to this battle that we call living, with its constant sorrow.

Can the sorrow in daily life end? Unless the mind changes radically, our living has very little meaning—going to the office every day, earning a livelihood, reading a few books, being able to quote cleverly, being very well informed—a life that is empty, a real bourgeois life. And then as one becomes aware of this state of affairs, one begins to invent a meaning to life, to find some significance to give to it. One searches out the clever people who will give one the significance, the purpose, of life—which is another escape from living. This kind of living must undergo a radical transformation.

Why is it we are frightened of death, as most people are? Frightened of what? Do please observe your own fears of what we call death, being frightened of coming to the end of this battle that we call living. We are frightened of the unknown, what might happen; we are frightened of leaving the known things, the family, the books, the attachment to our house and furniture, to the people near us. We are frightened to let go of the things known; and the known is this living in sorrow, pain, and despair, with occasional flashes of joy. There is no end to this constant struggle; that is what we call living; of that we are frightened to let go. Is it the "me"—who is the result of all this accumulation—that is frightened that it will come to an end; and therefore it demands a future hope; therefore there must be reincarnation? The idea of reincarnation—in which the whole of the East believes—is that you will be born in the next life a little higher up on the rungs of the ladder. You have been a dishwasher this life; next life you will be a prince, or whatever it is—somebody else will go and wash the dishes for you. For those who believe in reincarnation, what you are in this life matters very much, because what you do, how you behave, what your thoughts are, what your activities are, the next life is depending on this: you either get a reward or you are punished. But they do not care a pin about how they behave; for them it is just another form of belief, just as the belief that there is heaven, God, what you will. Actually all that matters is what you are now, today, how you actually behave, not only outwardly but also inwardly. The West has its own form of consolation about death; it rationalizes it; it has its own religious conditioning.

What is death, actually, the ending? The organism is going to end, because it grows old, or from disease and accident. Very few of us grow old beautifully, because we are tortured entities; our faces show it as we grow older—and there is the sadness of old age, remembering the things of the past.

Can one die to everything that is known psychologically, from day to day? Unless there is freedom from that known, what is possible can never be captured. As it is, our possibility is always within the field of the known; but when there is freedom, then that possibility is immense. Can one die, psychologically, to all one's past, to all the attachments, fears, to the anxiety, vanity, and pride, so completely that tomorrow one wakes up a fresh human being? You will say, "How is this to be done; what is the method?" There is no method, because a method implies tomorrow. It implies that you will practice and achieve something eventually, tomorrow, after many tomorrows. But can you see immediately the truth of it—see it actually, not theoretically—that the mind cannot be fresh, innocent, young, vital, passionate, unless there is an ending, psychologically, to everything of the past? But we do not want to let the past go because we *are* the past; all our thoughts are based on the past; all our knowledge is the past; so the mind cannot let go; any effort it makes to let go is still part of the past, the past hoping to achieve a different state.

The mind must become extraordinarily quiet, silent. And it does become extraordinarily quiet without any resistance, without any system, when it sees this whole issue. Man has always sought immortality. He paints a picture, puts his name on it. That is a form of immortality, leaving a name behind; man always wants to leave something of himself behind. What has he got to give—apart from technological knowledge—what has he of himself to give? What is he? You and I, what are we, psychologically? You may have a bigger bank account, be cleverer than I am, or this and that, but psychologically, what are we?—a lot of words, memories, experiences, and those we want to hand over to a son, put in a book, or paint in a picture. "Me." The "me" becomes extremely important: the "me" opposed to the community, the "me" wanting to identify itself, wanting to fulfill itself, wanting to become something great—you know, all the rest of it. When you observe that "me," you see that it is a bundle of memories, empty words. That is what we cling to; that is the very essence of the separation between "you" and "me," "they" and "we."

When you understand all this—observe it, not through another but through yourself, watch it very closely without any judgment, evaluation, suppression, just observe—then you will see that love is possible only when there is death. Love is not memory. Love is not pleasure. It is said that love is related to sex—back again to the division between profane love and sacred love, with approval of one and condemnation of the other. Surely love is none of these things. One cannot come upon it, totally, completely, unless there is a dying to the past, a dying to all the travail, conflict, and sorrow. Then there is love. Then one can do what one will.

Saanen

Do you mind inquiring into this whole question of what death is? A lot of people here are young people, and you may live very long, and there are a lot of old people here too, including myself; we are the people who are going, and you are the people who are coming. But you who are coming are going, and you also have to face death. So we are going to inquire into it; that is, we are going to have an insight into it. You cannot have an insight into it if there is any kind of fear, and fear comes only when you are attached to the things known. The things known are your images, your knowledge, your attachments, your furniture, your opinions, judgments, culture, your shyness, politeness—you follow—all that is the field of the known. If you are afraid, you will never have an insight into this whole problem of death.

I want to find out, as you must, what death is. Why am I frightened of death? Why am I so scared of old age and suddenly coming to an end? It is really a very complex business, the whole understanding of what death is, very complex. The very complexity of it makes one frightened because it is like very complex machinery; you dare not touch it, because you know nothing about it. But if you approach it very simply, which means really you are trying to learn about it, therefore you are enjoying it—not the idea of death but enjoying the investigation, the approach, the inquiry. Then you are learning, and you cannot learn if you are not happy; therefore you cannot have fear. That is the basic thing.

So if you really want to go into this, you have to be very clear that your mind, which means your thought, doesn't create fear, fear of what it considers coming to an end, what it considers entering into something it doesn't know.

Now first of all I have to find out—because I am not frightened, you understand, I am not interested in fear at all—if there is anything permanent as the "me." "Permanent" is that which has a continuity. I can leave my furniture to my brother, son, or whatever, and therefore it can remain in the family, or be sold in an antique shop and somebody else buys it. I want to find out if there is anything substantial, continuous, permanent as "me" who is frightened of death.

Is there anything permanent in me, in you?—permanent in the sense of continuity in time, a duration in space as the "me"? The "me" is the name—right? Has that name any permanence? Or does thought give permanence to the name? In itself it has no permanence, but thought, identifying itself with the body, with the image, with knowledge, with all the experiences, sorrows, pleasures, agonies, identifying itself with that, that gives it a quality of permanence. Otherwise is there anything permanent, a thing that has a continuity in spite of the non-existence of the body? Are you interested in all this? You are going to face this, whether you like it or not. Either you are going to face it accidentally, or through disease, or the natural decay of the organism. It is inevitable. You can avoid it by living longer, being healthier, taking more pills, and so on. But at the end there is this fact—unless I find out for myself if there is something permanent beyond death, which means timeless, which cannot be corrupted through civilization, through culture, something that in spite of all experience, knowledge, stimuli, reactions has its own existence and goes on as the "me." So man has said, "There is not the 'me,' but there is God." In Asia they put it differently, but it is still the act of thought that says, "There is the soul." It is an act of thought that says, "There is Brahman," as they say in India. It is still the act of thought, thought that is frightened of the unknown. Thought is the known, thought is time, thought is old, thought is never free. Because thought is the response of memory, experience, knowledge, therefore it is always old, never free, and being of time it is uncertain of the timeless, that is, beyond time. So it says, "I am not important; the 'me' is transient, is being put together by culture, by time, by accident, by the family, by tradition; it has developed certain tendencies, idiosyncrasies; it has its conditioning, but beyond all that there is the soul, there is something immense in me that is the permanent." All that is the process of thought. And thought, confronted with the inevitable, which is death, the ending, says, "I can't tolerate this"; therefore it says, "There must be a future life," or it says, "I believe there is a future life," or, "There is heaven, and I'll sit next to God"—it wants comfort faced with something completely unknown. And there are thousands of people who will give you comfort. All the organized churches offer that; you want that, and therefore they exist.

Now if you see how it is still the action of thought and is therefore based on fear, on imagination, on the past, that is the field of the known. That is, I am *attached* to the field of the known, with all its varieties, changes, its activities, and what I demand is comfort. Because I have found comfort in the past, I have lived within the field of the known; that is my territory, I know its borders, the frontiers. The frontiers are my consciousness, which is content. I am completely familiar with all that, and death is something I don't know; I don't want it.

So I ask myself: my life has been the past; I live in the past; I act in the past; that is my life. Listen to this! My life, living in the past, is a dead life. You understand? My mind, which lives in the past, is a dead mind. And thought says, "That is not death; the future is the death." So I see this as a fact. You follow? I see this as something enormously real. Therefore the mind, realizing that, actually dies to the past; it will use the past, but it has lost its grip; the past has lost its values, grip, its vitality. So the mind has its own energy, which is not derived from the past. Therefore living is dying—you understand? Therefore living is love, which is dying. Because if there is no attachment, then there is love. If there is no attachment to the past—the past has its value, which can be used, which must be used as knowledge—then my living is a constant renewal, is a constant movement in the field of the unknown in which there is learning, moving. Therefore death is the ultimate aloneness. And therefore there is a totally different kind of life.

Saanen

I would like to talk about an important question, which is that of death, death not only of the individual, but death as an idea that exists throughout the world and has been carried on as a problem for centuries without ever being resolved. There is not only the particular individual's fear of death but also an enormous, collective attitude toward death, in Asia as well as in the Western countries, which has to be understood. So we are going to consider together this whole issue.

In considering such a vast and significant problem, words are intended only to enable us to communicate, to have communion with each other. But the word itself can easily become a hindrance when we are trying to understand this profound question of death unless we give our *complete* attention to it, and not just verbally, flippantly, or intellectually try to find a reason for its existence.

Before, or perhaps in the process of, understanding this extraordinary thing called death, we shall have to understand also the significance of time, which is another great factor in our lives. Thought creates time, and time controls and shapes our thought. I am using the word *time* not only in the chronological sense of yesterday, today, and tomorrow but also in the psychological sense—the time that thought has invented as a means to arrive, to achieve, to postpone. Both are factors in our lives, are they not? One has to be aware of chronological time; otherwise you and I couldn't meet somewhere. Chronological time is obviously necessary in the events of our life; that is a simple, clear matter that need not be gone into very deeply. So what we have to explore, discuss, and understand is the whole *psychological* process that we call time.

Please, if you merely hear the words and do not see the implications behind the words, I am afraid we cannot go very far. Most of us are enslaved by words and by the concept of formula that the words have put together. Do not just brush this aside, because each one of us has a formula, a concept, an idea, an ideal—rational, irrational, or neurotic—according to which he is living. The mind is guiding itself by some pattern, by a particular series of words that have been made into a concept, a formula. This is true of each one of us, and please make no mistake about it—there is an idea, a pattern according to which we are shaping our lives. But if we are to understand this question of death and life, all formulas, patterns, and ideations—which exist because we do not understand living—must entirely go. A man who is living totally, completely, without fear has no *idea* about living. His action is thought, and his thought is action; they are not two separate things. But because we are afraid of the thing called death, we have divided it from life; we have put life and death into two separate watertight compartments with a great space between them, and we live according to the word, according to the formula of the past, the tradition of what has been. A mind that is caught in this process can never possibly see all the implications of death and of life or understand what truth is.

So when you inquire with me into this whole question, if you inquire as a Christian, a Buddhist, a Hindu, or what you will, you will be completely at a loss. And if you bring to this inquiry the residue of your various experiences, the knowledge that you have acquired from books, from other people, again you will be not only disappointed but also rather confused. The man who would really inquire must first be free of all these things, which make up his background—and that is our greatest difficulty. One must be free from the past, but not as a reaction, because without this freedom one cannot discover anything new. Understanding is freedom, but very few of us want to be free. We would rather live in a secure framework of our own making or in a framework put together by society. Any disturbance within that pattern is very disquieting, and rather than be disturbed we live a life of negligence, death, and decay.

To inquire into this enormous question of death, we must choicelessly be aware not only of our slavery to formulas and concepts but also of our fears, our desire for continuity, and so on. To inquire, we must come to the problem afresh. Please, this is really very important. The mind must be clear and not be caught in a concept or an idea if one would go into something that is quite extraordinary—as death must be. Death must be something extraordinary, not this thing that we try to cheat and are afraid of.

Psychologically we are slaves to time, time being the memory of yesterday, of the past, with all its accumulated experiences; it is not only your memory as that of a particular person but also the memory of the collective, of the race, of man throughout the ages. The past is made up of man's individual and collective sorrows, miseries, joys, his extraordinary struggle with life, with death, with truth, with society. All that is the past, yesterday multiplied by thousands; and for most of us the present is the movement of the past toward the future. There are not such exact divisions as the past, the present, and the future. What has been, modified by the present, is what will be. That is all we know. The future is the past modified by the accidents of the present; tomorrow is yesterday reshaped by the experiences, reactions, and knowledge of today. This is what we call time.

Time is a thing that has been put together by the brain, and the brain in turn is the result of time, of a thousand yesterdays. Every thought is the result of time; it is the response of memory, the reaction of yesterday's longings, frustrations, failures, sorrows, impending dangers; and with that background, we look at life, we consider everything. Whether there is God, or no God, what the function of the State is, the nature of relationship, how to overcome or to adjust oneself to jealousy, anxiety, guilt, despair, sorrow—we look at all these questions with that background of time.

Now whatever we look at with that background is distorted, and when the crisis demanding attention is very great, if we look at it with the eyes of the past, we either act neurotically, which is what most of us do, or we build for ourselves a wall of resistance against it. That is the whole process of our life.

Please, I am verbally exposing these things, but if you merely look at the words and do not observe your own process of thinking, which is to see yourself as you are, then you will not have a complete understanding of death; and there must be that understanding if you are to be free of fear and enter into something quite different.

We are everlastingly translating the present in terms of the past and thereby giving a continuity to what has been. For most of us the present is the continuation of the past. We meet the everyday happenings of our life—which always have their own newness, their own significance—with the dead weight of the past, thereby creating that which we call the future. If you have observed your own mind, not only the conscious but also the unconscious, you will know that it is the past, that there is nothing in it that is new, nothing that is not corrupted by the past, by time. And there is what we call the present. Is there a present untouched by the past? Is there a present that does not condition the future?

Probably you have not thought about this before, and we shall have to go into it a little bit. Most of us just want to live in the present because the past is so heavy, so burdensome, so inexhaustible, and the future so uncertain. The modern mind says, "Live completely in the present. Don't bother about what will happen tomorrow, but live for today. Life is such a misery anyhow, and the evil of one day is enough; so live each day completely and forget everything else." That is obviously a philosophy of despair.

Is it possible to live in the present without bringing time into it, which is the past? Surely you can live in that totality of the present only when you understand the whole of the past. To die to time is to live in the present, and you can die to time only if you have understood the past, which is to understand your own mind—not only the conscious mind that goes to the office every day, gathers knowledge and experience, has superficial reactions, and all the rest of it, but also the unconscious mind, in which are buried the accumulated traditions of the family, of the group, of the race. Buried in the unconscious also are the enormous sorrow of man and the fear of death. All that is the past, which is yourself, and you have to understand it. If you do not understand *that*, if you have not inquired into the ways of your own mind and heart, into your greed and sorrow, if you do not know yourself *completely*, you cannot live in the present. To live in the present is to die to the past. In the process of understanding yourself, you are made free of the past, which is your conditioning—your conditioning as a Communist, a Catholic, a Protestant, a Hindu, a Buddhist, the conditioning imposed upon you by society, and by your own greeds, envies, anxieties, despairs, sorrows, and frustrations. It is your conditioning that gives continuity to the "me," the self.

If you do not know yourself, your unconscious as well as your conscious state, all your inquiry will be twisted, given a bias. You will have no foundation for thinking that is rational, clear, logical, sane. Your thinking will be according to a certain pattern, formula, or set of ideas, but that is not really thinking. To think clearly, logically, without becoming neurotic, without being caught in any form of illusion, you have to know this whole process of your own consciousness, which is put together by time, by the past. And is it possible to live without the past? Surely that is death. Do you understand? We will come back to the question of the present when we have seen for ourselves what death is.

What is death? This is a question for the young and for the old, so please put it to yourself. Is death merely the ending of the physical organism? Is that what we are afraid of? Is it the body that we want to continue? Or is it some other form of continuance that we crave? We all realize that the body, the physical entity, wears out through use, through various pressures, influences, conflicts, urges, demands, sorrows. Some would probably like it if the body could be made to continue for 150 years or more, and perhaps the doctors and scientists together will ultimately find some way of prolonging the agony in which most of us live. But sooner or later the body dies; the physical organism comes to an end. Like any machine, it eventually wears out.

For most of us, death is something much deeper than the ending of the body, and all religions promise some kind of life beyond death. We crave continuity; we want to be assured that something continues when the body dies. We hope that the psyche, the "me"—the "me" that has experienced, struggled, acquired, learned, suffered, enjoyed; the "me," which in the West is called the soul and by another name in the East—will continue. So what we are concerned with is continuity, not death. We do not want to know what death is; we do not want to know the extra-ordinary miracle, the beauty, the depth, the vastness of death. We don't want to inquire into that something that we don't know. All we want is to continue. We say, "I who have lived for forty, sixty, eighty years; I who have a house, a family, children, and grandchildren; I who have gone to the office day after day for so many years; I who have had quarrels, sexual appetites; I want to go on living." That is all we are concerned with. We know that there is death, that the ending of the physical body is inevitable, so we say, "I must feel assured of the continuity of myself after death." So we have beliefs, dogmas, resurrection, reincarnation—a thousand ways of escaping from the reality of death. And when we have a war, we put up crosses for the poor chaps who have been killed off. This sort of thing has been going on for millennia.

We have never really given our whole being to finding out what death is. We always approach death with the condition that we must be assured of a continuity hereafter. We say, "I want the known to continue," the known being our qualities, our capacities, the memory of our experiences, our struggles, fulfillments, frustrations, ambitions; and it is also our name and property. All that is the known, and we want it all to continue. Once we are granted the certainty of that continuance, then perhaps we may inquire into what death is and whether there is such a thing as the unknown—which must be something extraordinary to find out.

So you see the difficulty. What we want is continuance, and we have never asked ourselves what it is that makes for continuance, that gives rise to this chain, this movement of continuity. If you observe, you will see that it is thought alone that gives a sense of continuance—nothing else. Through thought you identify yourself with your family, with your house, with your pictures or poems, with your character, with your frustrations, with your joys. The more you think about a problem, the more you give root and continuance to that problem. If you like someone, you think about that person, and this very thought gives a sense of continuity in time. Obviously, you have to think, but can you think for the moment, *at* the moment—and then drop thinking? If you did not say, "I like this, it is mine—it is my picture, my self-expression, my God, my wife, my virtue—and I am going to keep it," you would have no sense of continuity in time. But you don't think clearly, right through every problem. There are always the pleasure that you want to keep and the pain that you want to get rid of, which means that you think about both, and thought gives continuity to both. What we call thought is the response of memory, of association, which is essentially the same as the response of a computer. You have to come to the point where you see for yourself the truth of this.

Most of us do not really want to find out for ourselves what death is; on the contrary, we want to continue in the known. If my brother, my son, my wife, or my husband dies, I am miserable, lonely, self-pitying, which is what I call sorrow, and I live on in that messy, confused, miserable state. I divide death from life, the life of quarrels, bitterness, despair, disappointments, frustrations, humiliations, insults, because this life I know, and death I don't know. Belief and dogma satisfy me till I die. That is what takes place for most of us.

This sense of continuity that thought gives to consciousness is quite shallow, as you can see. There is nothing mysterious or ennobling about it, and when you understand the whole significance of it, you think—where thought is necessary—clearly, logically, sanely, unsentimentally, without this constant urge to fulfil, to be or to become somebody. Then you will know how to live in the present, and living in the present is dying from moment to moment. You are then able to inquire, because your mind, being unafraid, is without any illusion. To be without any illusion is absolutely necessary, and illusion exists only as long as there is fear. When there is no fear, there is no illusion. Illusion arises when fear takes root in security, whether it be in the form of a particular relationship, a house, a belief, or position and prestige. Fear creates illusion. As long as fear continues, the mind will be caught in various forms of illusion, and such a mind cannot possibly understand what death is.

We are now going to inquire into what death is—at least, I will inquire into it, expose it. But you can understand death, live with it completely, know the deep, full significance of it, only when there is no fear and therefore no illusion. To be free of fear is to live completely in the present, which means that you are not functioning mechanically in the habit of memory. Most of us are concerned about reincarnation, or we want to know whether we continue to live after the body dies, which is all so trivial. Have we understood the triviality of this desire for continuity? Do we see that it is merely the process of thinking, the machine of thought that demands to continue? Once you see that fact, you realize the utter shallowness, the stupidity of such a demand. Does the "I" continue after death? Who cares? And what is this "I" that you want to continue? Your pleasures and dreams, your hopes, despairs, and joys, your property and the name you bear, your petty little character, and the knowledge you have acquired in your cramped, narrow life, which has been added to by professors, by literary people, by artists. *That* is what you want to continue, and that is all.

Now, whether you are old or young, you have to finish with all that. You have to finish with it completely, surgically, as a surgeon operates with a knife. Then the mind is without illusion and without fear; therefore it can observe and understand what death is. Fear exists because of the desire to hold on to what is known. The known is the past living in the present and modifying the future. That is our life day after day, year after year, till we die. How can such a mind understand something that has no time, no motive, something totally unknown?

Do you understand? Death is the unknown, and you have ideas about it. You avoid looking at death, or you rationalize it, saying it is inevitable, or you have a belief that gives you comfort, hope. But it is only a mature mind, a mind that is without fear, without illusion, without this stupid search for self-expression and continuity—it is only such a mind that can observe and find out what death is, because it knows how to live in the present.

Please follow this. To live in the present is to be without despair, because there is no hankering after the past, and there is no hope in the future. Therefore the mind says, "Today is enough for me." It does not avoid the past or blind itself to the future, but it has understood the totality of consciousness, which is not only the individual but also the collective; and therefore there is no "me" separate from the many. In understanding the totality of itself, the mind has understood the particular as well as the universal. Therefore it has cast aside ambition, snobbishness, social prestige; all that is completely gone from a mind that is living wholly in the present and therefore dying to everything it has known, every minute of the day. Then you will find, if you have gone that far, that death and life are one. You are living totally in the present, completely attentive, without choice, without effort; the mind is always empty, and from that emptiness you look, you observe, you understand, and therefore living is dying. What has continuity can never be creative. Only that which ends can know what it is to create. When life is also death, there is love, there is truth, there is creation; because death is the unknown, as truth and love and creation are.

Do you want to ask any questions and discuss?

Questioner: Is dying an act of will, or is it the unknown itself?

Krishnamurti: Sir, have you ever died to your pleasure— just died to it without arguing, without reacting, without trying to create special conditions, without asking how you are to give it up, or why you should give it up? Have you ever done that? You will have to do that when you die physically, won't you? One can't argue with death. One can't say to death, "Give me a few more days to live." There is no effort of will in dying—one just dies. Or have you ever died to any of your despairs, your ambitions— just given it up, put it aside, as a leaf that dies in the autumn, without any battle of will, without anxiety as to what will happen to you if you do? Have you? I am afraid you have not. When you leave here now, die to something that you cling to—your habit of smoking, your sexual demand, your urge to be famous as an artist, as a poet, as this or that. Just give it up, just brush it aside as you would some stupid thing, without effort, without choice, without decision. If your dying to it is total—and not just the giving up of cigarettes or of drinking, which you make into a tremendous issue—you will know what it means to live in the moment supremely, effortlessly, with all your being. And then, perhaps, a door may open into the unknown.

7 September 1974

Brockwood Park

You know, death has been one of the problems, probably the greatest problem, in human life. Not love, not fear, not relationship, but this question, this mystery, this sense of ending, has been the concern from ancient times. Here, we are trying to investigate what that thing is. Can we investigate what death is when we have separated it from living? You understand my question? I have separated death as something at the end of my life—right?— something that I have postponed, put away, a long interval between the living and the dying. Dying is something in the future, something of which one is frightened, something that one doesn't want, to be totally avoided. But it is always there. Whether through accident, disease, or old age, it is always there. Whether we are young or old, infirm or full of joy, it is always there. People have said, "Living is only a means to dying; death is much more important than living; look to death rather than to life." Knowing that there is death, people have invented every form of comfort— comfort in belief, in ideals, in hopes that you will sit "on the right hand of God" when you behave properly, and so on, and on, and on. The whole of Asia believes in reincarnation. Here, you have not such a rationalized hope but a sentimental hope.

When you look at all this—the beliefs, the comforts, the desire for comfort, knowing that there is an ending, the hope that next life you will continue, and the whole intellectual rationalization of death—you see that you have separated dying from living. Dying is separated from living, everyday living with all the conflicts, the miseries, the attachments, the despairs, the anxieties, the violence, the suffering, the tears, and the laughter. Why has the mind separated life from dying? The life that we lead, the everyday life, the shoddiness of it, the bitterness of it, the emptiness of it, the travail, the routine, the office year in and year out for fifty years or more, going to the factory, all that we call living. The strife, the struggle, the ambition, the corruption, the fleeting affections and joys and pleasures: that is what we call living. And we say death mustn't enter into that field because that is all we know, and death we do not know; therefore keep it away. So we cling to the known—please watch it in yourself—to the known, to the remembrance of things past, to the sorrows, to the anxieties, to memories, to experiences, which are all the known and therefore the past. We cling to the past, and that is what we call the known. And the unknown is death, of which you are frightened. So there is a wide gulf between the known and the unknown. We would rather cling to the known than enter into the field of the unknown because our minds operate always within the known, because there there is security. We *think* there is security, we *think* there is certainty, we *think* there is permanence; and when you look at it, it is impermanent, it is totally uncertain. Yet we cling to it because that is all we know. That is, we only know the past.

And death is something we do not know. Now this division exists, and it exists because thought has divided life as living, dying, love, and all the rest of it. Thought has divided the artist, the businessman, the Socialist, the politician. Thought has divided life into the known and death as something unknown. These are all facts.

Now can the mind, which clings to the known, inquire into what is permanent? Because that is what we think we are clinging to: the permanent relationship between you and another, the permanent ownership of land, property, money, name, form, idea. Now is there anything permanent—not as an idea but as an actuality? Please work at it! Is there anything permanent— "my name, my reputation, my house, my wife, my children, my ideals, my experience"? Yet the mind wants permanence because in that there is security. So realizing there is nothing permanent here, *nothing*, it creates a permanence in God, in an idea; and you find how extraordinarily difficult it is for human beings to change ideas. That is our battle now, between you and the speaker, because you have ideals, or ideas, or pictures, images that you think are permanent. You have accepted the permanence as real. Then along comes somebody who says, "Look, there is nothing permanent. Your ideas, your gods, your saviors, you yourself are impermanent," and you refuse to see that. To realize that there is impermanence, uncertainty, creates havoc in one's life. The more uncertain you are, the more neurotic you become, the more imbalanced; the more insane the world is, so your activities become. So you must have something permanent, and so you create a belief, a god, an ideal, a conclusion, an image. These are all illusions, because there is nothing permanent, but yet unless the mind has something basically permanent, all its activities will be distorted, neurotic, incomplete. *Is* there something totally permanent? You are following all this? For God's sake follow it; it is your life!

If there is nothing permanent, then life becomes totally meaningless. So is there something permanent—not a house or an idea—but something that is beyond and above this impermanence? We are investigating that. You have to follow this a little bit carefully; otherwise you will miss it.

We live in the past, and the past has become our permanence, our state of permanence. When you observe and see the illusion of the past, what comes out of that perception? I see that living in the past has certain values: I can't ride a bicycle, I can't speak English, or drive a car, or do certain technological things, or recognize you, my friend, or my wife, children, without the knowledge of the past. But is there a quality of mind that is not put together by thought that in itself is impermanent? Is there a quality out of this perception? That quality is intelligence. That intelligence is not yours or mine. It is intelligence, the intelligence that is capable of seeing the impermanent and of not going off into neurotic habits or activities. Because it is intelligence, it is always acting rightly. Got it?

With that intelligence we are now going to look at death. We say death is something unknown. Being attached to all the things that we know, what we are frightened of is complete ending of that attachment: attachment to my name, attachment to my family, to my job, to the book I have written, to the book I hope to write, or to the picture of God knows what else, various forms of attachment. Death is the ending of that attachment. Right? Now living, daily, can you be free of attachment, therefore inviting death? You understand what I am talking about? You have understood? Am I making myself clear? That is, I am attached to my book, to my reputation, to my family, to my job, to my pride, to my vanity, to my sense of honesty, to my sense of glory, or whatever it is that I am attached to. Death means the ending of that attachment. Now can I end that attachment immediately—which *is* death? So I have brought death into the very moment of living. So there is no fear. When the mind sees the truth of this—that death is an ending of the things that you are attached to, whether it is to the furniture, to your face, to ideals, and so on—you have brought this faraway thing called death to the immediate action of life, which is the ending of your attachment. So death means a total renewal—do you understand?—a total renewal of a mind that has been caught in the past. So the mind becomes astonishingly alive; it is not living in the past.

If the mind is capable of this action, and it is tremendous action, to end completely every day to all the things that one is attached to, every day and every minute you are living with life and death together.

From this arises the problem: If you cannot do it, what will happen? Do you understand? My son can't do this, or my friend, my brother, can't do this; you have done it, and I can't do it. You have applied, you are diligent, you are attentive, you have understood this thing basically, radically, that you are not dependent any more on anything. Ending all that dependency, that attachment, *immediately*: that is death. Then what happens to those who do not enter into that intelligence, supreme excellence of action?

You know most people live in the past, live thoughtlessly, live without sanity. What happens to all those people? You have stepped out of that stream of life, which means you are compassionate, you know what you are doing, are aware of the significance of the past, the present, and the future, all that is involved. And I am not. I don't even listen to you, I don't even care, I just want to have a good time, I want to enjoy myself, that is all my concern. I may be afraid of death, and I have a comforting belief that I will be born again next life, or that I will end up in heaven. So what happens to me? What is your relationship to me? You, who have understood all this, are therefore compassionate, and your actions are supremely intelligent and therefore excellent, and I am not interested in what you are saying, doing, writing, thinking; I am caught in this stream, as most human beings are. Very few step out of that stream. What is your relationship to the man in the stream? Have you any relationship, or none at all? How can you have any relationship with the insane when you are sane? You can be compassionate, you can be kind, generous, and all the rest of it, but you have no relationship. Therefore what can you do?

Your responsibility, then, is, if you are out of that stream, to live that life. Not be an *example!* If you are an example, then you become a dead person; then you have a following; then you become the authority; then you are the very essence of destruction, you are the very cause of that stream. Then what will you do? You have a responsibility to act intelligently. Because you have seen the whole issue, the perception of the map of the whole thing that we have talked about brings that intelligence, and according to that intelligence you will act. Not "I like" or "I don't like." That is the responsibility.

30 July 1976

Saanen

Krishnamurti: If you want to, let's discuss death. It is an immense problem, you understand. Do you really want to go into it?

We are going to have a dialogue about death—dialogue being a conversation, an inquiry between two friends, between two people, or a few people, who are really concerned about it, not theoretically, who actually want to find out. So we are inquiring; we are not dogmatically stating anything. When we inquire rightly, then we discover the truth of it. To inquire correctly, there must be freedom. If I am afraid of death, then I can't inquire, because that fear is going to warp my investigation. Is that clear? Or if I have a belief about death and an afterlife, that too distorts investigation.

To investigate about a human problem, as death, which is very complex, there must be freedom to look. You cannot observe or investigate if there is any kind of prejudice, belief, hope, fear. To inquire very seriously there must be no prejudice that distorts, no fear, no desire for comfort, hope, none of that. The mind must be completely empty to look. That is the first thing to have, to find out about something.

Every human being has a desire for continuity. The ancient Egyptians did it in one way, and modern people do it another way; they bury them or incinerate them, but they hope something will continue. There is this solid demand on the part of every human being that there must be some kind of continuity. Right? It is there in you, isn't it? Look at it. So what is it that continues? Is there anything that continues? Is there anything permanent? Or is everything impermanent? You understand my questions? I must find that out. Before I can go into the question of death, I, or you, a human being, must first find out if there is anything permanent that continues. Continuity implies permanence. Now is there anything in you as a human being that has a continuity?

Questioner: There is a desire for continuing.

Krishnamurti: No, sir, careful. Apart from desire, is there anything permanent—permanent being continuous, which is a movement without an end?

Questioner: Maybe.

Krishnamurti: No, not maybe. First look at it. There is the desire for continuity—desire being sensation, then thought as desire, and the desire creates the image. See the sequence of it—sensation, thought, desire, the image making. Apart from desire, is there something that is permanent, which means time doesn't touch it? That is what we mean by permanent: time will not change it, and therefore it is a movement continuously. Is there anything in a human being that is permanent?

Questioner: Continuity implies time.

Krishnamurti: That's right, sir. Continuity means time, and also it means there is no time. If it is continuous from the beginning, never ending, it is beyond time. Just a minute. I don't want to investigate that yet. Is there anything in a human being, in you, in me, that is permanent?

Questioner: There is a feeling of existence, of the self.

Krishnamurti: There is the feeling of existence; there is the feeling of the self—the self and the feeling of living, from childhood until you die—existence, the feeling of living. He said the "I" is permanent; somebody said that. So what is the "I," the "me"? The psyche, the personality, what is that? Please, be serious! Don't fiddle with this thing; it is much too serious if you really want to go into this question.

Questioner: Thought as memory.

Krishnamurti: You are saying thought as memory. Are you repeating this because you have heard somebody say it, or is it a truth to you? Please, sir, do listen carefully. We are having a conversation, or inquiring into what is the "I"—the "I" being the feeling that you are living, that you are existing. Now what is the "I"? Is that "I" permanent? The ancient Hindus laid down that the "I" is evolving, life after life, until it reaches perfection, which is the highest principle, Brahman. So that "I" has a continuity till it makes itself perfect and is absorbed into the highest principle. That is the idea of reincarnation. Reincarnating—please listen to that word *reincarnating*, that is, born over again. Now we are asking, what is that "I"? Is that "I" permanent? Don't repeat something that you do not yourself find. Then you are merely repeating what somebody else has said. That is of no value. Is that "I" permanent? Which means, what is that "I"? How does it come into being? Is it a spiritual entity, therefore continuous, or is it a momentary affair, in a flux, in constant change? Is it in essence a spiritual thing that is a non-material process? Or is it a material process? Material process being thought as being matter built through various incidents, accidents, impressions, impingements of environment, family. All that is a material process put together by thought. Thought says, "I am different from thought." The "I" and thought have separated themselves and said, "Thought will go on; my thought will go on." Right?

You have to find out for yourself, in this inquiry about death, if there is anything permanent, or if everything is in movement. Everything, both the material process and the idea that you are a spirit, both are in constant movement—movement being time, time being from here to there, chronologically, time also being the cultivation of the psyche. Movement; so is there anything permanent, or is everything in a human being undergoing change?

Questioner: *Something is permanent.*

Krishnamurti: He says we are something permanent, that there are certain moments in life when there is a realization or a happening that is beyond time, and that happening is permanent. That is what the gentleman says. When that thing happens, if it has become a memory...

Questioner: *It isn't a memory, sir.*

Krishnamurti: Wait, listen. I said *if* it has become a memory, then it is a material process, and you can call that permanent. If that extraordinary state of timelessness happens, and if it is not a memory, the question then is: Will it continue? That is, you have an experience of something—I won't use even the word *experience*—a happening of something that is beyond time; when it is not registered as a memory, it still remains beyond time. The moment it is registered, it is made of time. That is simple. Then is that happening a continuous thing? Or does it end? If it is continuous, then it is of time. Please, I have gone into this very carefully because we are going to go into something that requires great attention, real sensitivity to find out. We are asking, is there something permanent? It is for you to answer.

Questioner: We want something to be permanent.

Krishnamurti: There is the desire to have permanence—my permanent house, my permanent name, my permanent form; the memories, the attachment, we want everything permanent. All insurance is based on permanence. We have to find out for ourselves if there is anything permanent.

Do look, please. For myself, there is nothing permanent—I am not imposing this on you—nothing is permanent. Then what is death if there is a continuity of the "me," the "me" with its structure put together by thought, thought being the word, the word being the name, the name being attached to the form? The name, the form of this body, the organism, and the whole structure of the psyche, is put together by thought, obviously. Do you see that? Or do you say, "No, no, there is something much more spiritual behind that"? If there is something much more spiritual behind that, and if you say that exists, it is still part of thought. You understand? If you say that behind the veil of time— which is a good expression—there is something utterly timeless, then you have recognized it; right? If you have recognized it, it is part of your memory. If it is a memory, it is a material process of thought. If that something behind the veil is real, true, therefore unthinkable, you don't *know*. When you assert there is something spiritual, a spiritual essence, you have already contaminated it; therefore it is no longer spiritual. Grasp this once, and you will see. You see this is an old trick of a great many of the Hindus, that there is God, Brahman, within you, and all you have to do is to peel off, like onion skins. You understand? That is: you have established a God in you by thought, and then thought says, "I must get at it; therefore let me operate."

So if all thought is a material process, and whatever it has put together is still a material process, even though it says, "There is a permanent me," it is still part of the structure of thought. Then what is an ending, which is death? I wonder if you are following all this. Just listen to this, look at it, don't answer me, look before you answer it. As most of us desire continuity and therefore are frightened of death, then what takes place when there is an ending called death?

Let me put it very simply. An ordinary human being says, "I must continue. I am frightened of death." But there *is* an ending. I die. I may not want to die. I may cry at death, I may fight against death, but it is inevitable. So I am saying, when there is the desire for continuity and there is an ending, then what takes place?

There is the death of the organism, and there is the death of the psyche. They are interrelated, psychosomatic, all that business. A man says, "I must continue. I want to continue; it's my life. For God's sake help me, because my one desire is to continue." And I am asking, "All right, my friend, what happens when that end comes, which is inevitable? It ends through accident, through disease, all kinds of endings, what happens? To find out what happens, you must investigate if the psyche, the 'me,' is a permanent thing, or an impermanent thing. If it is impermanent, then in the ending what happens?" Please, don't answer! Look at it! Find out for yourself! This is tremendously important because man says, "I must find immortality." The ancient Egyptians found immortality in the tombs through a continuity of their daily life eternally. If you have looked at the Egyptian tombs and read about them, you know that that was their desire, that they must continue for the next thousand years or million years. The Nile Valley was protected—desert on both sides—and it gave the Egyptians a sense of permanence, and that permanence they translated as continuous life. You can read about it, or, if you are interested, you can look at it. And the ancient Hindus said the self, though it is impermanent, must continue until it reaches the perfect principle, the highest principle, which is Brahman. Or they said there is God in you, and through various incarnations you will make the ego perfect until it reaches the highest principle. And the Christians have their own way, resurrection and all the rest of it.

Now I want to find out, as a human being; though my desire is for continuity, I know there is inevitably death. Inevitably, whether you like it or not, it is there. And I say to myself, what happens when there is an ending?

Questioner: *It is a great shock.*

Krishnamurti: That's not my question, please. We will discuss it in a different way. You are not answering my question because you are not facing it; you are not looking at it, not putting your teeth into it to find out.

"I want to continue; that is my hope, my desire, my longing. I have continued for eighty years with my family, with my furniture, with my books, with all the things I have collected for eighty years, and please give me another thousand years with the same things." But death comes along and says, "No, my friend, you are going to die." What happens after that? Human beings desire a continuity, and there is an ending. Continuity is all that the human mind has collected: knowledge, things, ideas, attachments, property, beliefs, gods. All that I want to continue for the rest of eternity. But death comes and says, "End it." So I am asking, what is it that ends?

Questioner: *The psyche.*

Krishnamurti: Are you sure? Sir, be careful; don't just speculate. I really don't like to discuss this or go into it with many people, because they are not serious. This demands great seriousness, not just verbalizing all the time. I said, the desire comes into being through sensation and thought; then thought, which is desire, has a name, as K, the form of K, and there is all the content of my consciousness, which has been put together by thought, that I want to continue. I want thought with all its content, with all the attachments, with all the pain, with all the suffering, with all the misery and confusion; *that* I want to continue.

When the physical body dies, the material process, which is the brain structure, which is the thought process, dies. You understand? I wonder if you see this.

Questioner: *(inaudible)*

Krishnamurti: Sir, I am the world, and the world is me. That is a fact. Right? The world is me, not as an idea, not as a theory, but as an actuality. That I am the world and the world is me is as real a fact as the fact that if I put a pin in myself there is pain. The "me" is put together by thought. It is a material process. Thought is matter, a material process, because it is the response of memory, which is stored in the brain as knowledge, and so when that brain dies, the material process dies. Then what takes place? You understand my question?

Questioner: *That material process dies.*

Krishnamurti: Madame, if I may point out without being rude, when you say the material process dies, have you died to that *now*? Not when death comes. Do you understand? I'll show it to you.

I am the world, and the world is me. My consciousness is the consciousness of the world. The content of my consciousness is the content of the consciousness of the world. That content is put together by thought—my furniture, my name, my family, my bank account, my belief, my dogmas—all that is in my consciousness, which is the world's consciousness. Unless you see that, you can't go further into what we are inquiring about. Then that consciousness, which is a material process, comes to an end, because the organism collapses through disease, accident, and so on; so the brain decays, and so the thought process comes to an end. The thought process, which has put together the ego, the "me," has come to an end. Ah, you don't accept that. So I say, is it possible to die now to everything that thought has put together as consciousness, which is me, and the world? I wonder if you understand my question.

Questioner: *We can't accept what you say. That is annihilation.*

Krishnamurti: He says, "We can't accept that because it means total annihilation." That we can't accept; why not, if that is true? That's why you want something permanent. You want something that will be endless, which is yourself, with all your miseries, all that business. So I say to myself, "As I am the world and the world is me, my consciousness is the consciousness of the world, and all the content of that consciousness, which makes up consciousness, is put together by thought; beliefs, dogmas, rituals, everything is put together by thought." I say to myself, "Can all that die now, not fifty years later, *now*?" Which means, can that content empty itself now? You understand? That is, death is *now*, not fifty years later.

When you die, your body withers away and your brain ends. And all the content of your consciousness cannot continue as it is because it is the thought process. So I am asking myself, and you—I am asking *you*, not myself, I am asking you as a human being—seeing the reason of all this, the logic, and therefore going beyond logic, the truth of it, that you are the world and the world is you, and that your consciousness is the consciousness of the world, when you see that, have an insight into that, then can all the things that have been put together by thought come to an end, not fifty years later, but *now*? Have you understood my question? Please, this is dreadfully serious.

Look, sir, part of my consciousness is, I believe. Belief is part of my consciousness. Right through the world they believe in something: in God, in the perfect State, in my experience, in Jesus, in Buddha. To believe is a common factor of man. That belief is put together by thought, which is a material process. Can you end that belief *now* as you are going to do when you die? You follow? End your belief in something immediately, and see what takes place, not say, "I am frightened to drop my beliefs, because beliefs give me tremendous security." You are seeking security in illusion; therefore it is no security at all. Can you die to that now? Only then can you answer what comes next. But before you can answer what comes next, you must act. Words are not action; theories are not action. When there is this perception that belief is one of the most common factors of human desire—and it *is* an illusion because it is put together by thought—can I die to that?

Can you die to belief, not to a particular belief, but to *belief*? Most people have ideals, and it is a most extraordinary phenomenon that wherever you go in the world every human being has ideals; it doesn't matter what it is, noble, ignoble, actual, and so on. Now ideas are obviously put together by thought; it is a material process in opposition to what I *am*. So can you die to that?

Unless you die to that, you cannot possibly answer the next question, which we want to find out before we die. That's what we are clinging to, you understand. If that can be told, verbalized, and then made common, you will all believe in that. It becomes vulgar—I am using the word *vulgar* in the ordinary sense, common, not derogatory, insulting. Then it becomes a belief, and we are all happy. But to die not knowing—you understand? No, you don't understand. We are only dealing with facts, not with theories, not with projected ideas, comforting or ennobling; we are dealing with actual facts of daily life. Our daily life is made up of things put together by thought. Thought is a material process.

Let me put it another way. A human being doesn't end his sorrows, his miseries, his confusion. Then he is like the rest of the world. He dies, but sorrow, confusion, misery, as a vast field, goes on. This is a fact. Like a vast volume of water in a great river, there is this immense sorrow of man. For God's sake, do see all this. There is such violence, hatred, jealousy; that is the vast stream. We human beings are part of that stream. Unless I die to that stream, it will go on; the stream, which is the world, will go on. So the man who steps out of the stream, the human being who steps out of the stream, will know what is beyond what is. But as long as you remain in that stream, one foot in and one foot out, playing—which most of us do—you will never find out what is beyond death. Which means one must die to everything without hope. You understand all this? That is one of the most difficult things. A man who dies to everything will know what is eternal. You understand?

Questioner: *(inaudible)*

Krishnamurti: Sir, you go back into theories.

Look, you see sir, please. You know it is one of the most difficult things to talk or discuss, or go into things with tremendous attention right to the end. Only very few people can do it. This is a subject that demands all your attention, not verbalization, theories, and all that, but continuous attention. Few can do this; few want to do this. They can do it, but they are too lazy, too uninterested. If you are really captivated, caught by this, wanting to find out, you will give complete attention, therefore no words, but constant pushing, pushing, pushing, not knowing where you are going. And that is death. When you die, there is an ending to everything that you know. So can you not die now to everything that you know? Then you will find out for yourself what is truth in which there is no illusion, nothing personal. It is not my truth or your truth. It is truth.

Madras

Is it possible to live with a sense of harmony, beauty, with a sense of never-ending fulfillment—or rather, I won't say fulfillment because fulfillment brings frustration—but is there a never-ending state of action in which there is no sorrow, no repentance, no cause for regret? If there is such a state, then how is one to come to it? One obviously cannot cultivate it. One cannot say, "I shall be harmonious"; it means nothing. To assume that one must control oneself in order to be harmonious is an immature way of thinking. The state of total integration, of unitary action, can come only when one is not seeking it, when the mind is not forcing itself into a patterned way of living.

Most of us have not given much thought to all this. In our daily activities we are concerned only with time, because time helps us to forget; time heals our wounds, however temporarily; time dissipates our despairs, our frustrations. Being caught in the time process, how is one to come upon this extraordinary state in which there is no contradiction, in which the very movement of living is integrated action, and everyday life is reality? If each one of us seriously puts this question to himself, then I think we shall be able to commune with each other in unfolding the problem; but if you are merely listening to words, then you and I are not in communion. We are in communion with each other only if this is a problem to both of us. Then it is not just my problem, which I am imposing on you or which you are trying to interpret according to your beliefs and idiosyncrasies. This is a human problem, and world problem, and if it is very clear to each one of us, then what I am saying, what I am thinking and feeling, will bring about a state of communion between us, and together we can go to great depths.

So what is the problem? The problem is that there must obviously be a tremendous change, not only at the superficial level, in one's outward activities, but inwardly, deeply; there must be an inner revolution that will transform the manner of one's thinking and bring about a way of life that in itself is total action. And why doesn't such a revolution take place? That is the problem as one sees it. So let us go deeply into ourselves and discover the root of this problem.

The root of the problem is fear, is it not? Please look into it for yourselves and don't just regard me as a speaker addressing an audience. I want to go into this problem with you because, if you and I explore it together, and we both understand something that is true, then from that understanding there will be an action that is neither yours nor mine, and opinions, over which we battle everlastingly, will have ceased to exist.

I feel there is a basic fear that has to be discovered—a fear much more profound than the fear of losing one's job, or the fear of going wrong, or the fear of outward or inward insecurity. But to go into it very deeply, we must begin with the fears that we know, the fears of which we are all conscious. I do not have to tell you what they are, for you can observe them in yourselves: the fear of public opinion, the fear of losing one's son, one's wife, or one's husband through the sad experience called death, the fear of disease, the fear of loneliness, the fear of not being successful, of not fulfilling oneself, the fear of not attaining to a knowledge of truth, God, heaven, or what you will. The savage has a few very simple fears, but we have innumerable fears whose complexity increases as we become more and more "civilized."

Now what is fear? Have you ever actually experienced fear? You may lose your job, you may not be a success, your neighbor may say this or that of you, and death is always waiting just around the corner. All this breeds fear in you, and you run away from it through yoga, through reading books, through belief in God, through various forms of amusement, and all the rest of it. So I am asking: Have you ever really experienced fear, or does the mind always run away from it?

Take the fear of death. Being afraid of death, you rationalize your fear away by saying that death is inevitable, that everything dies. The rationalizing process is merely an escape from the fact. Or you believe in reincarnation, which satisfies, comforts you, but fear is still there. Or you try to live totally in the present, to forget all about the past and the future, and to be concerned only with the now, but fear goes on.

I am asking you whether you have ever known real fear—not the theoretical fear that the mind merely conceives of. Perhaps I am not making it very clear. You know the taste of salt. You have experienced pain, lust, envy, and you know for yourselves what these words mean. In the same way, do you know fear? Or have you only an *idea* of what fear is without having actually experienced fear? Am I explaining myself?

You are afraid of death, and what is that fear? You see the inevitability of death, and because you do not want to die, you are afraid of it. But you have never known what death is; you have only projected an opinion, an idea about it. So you are afraid of an idea about death. This is rather simple, and I do not quite understand our difficulty.

To really experience fear, you must be totally *with* it; you must be entirely *in* it and not avoid it; you cannot have beliefs, opinions about it. But I do not think many of us have ever experienced fear in this way because we are always avoiding, running away from fear. We never remain with it, look into it, find out what it is all about.

Is the mind capable of living with fear, being a part of it? Can the mind go into that feeling instead of avoiding it or trying to escape from it? I think it is largely because we are always running away from fear that we live such contradictory lives.

Sirs, one is aware, especially as one grows older, that death is always waiting. And you are afraid of death, aren't you? Now, how are you to understand that fear? How are you to be free from the fear of death? What is death? It is really the ending of everything you have known. That is the actual fact. Whether or not you survive is not the point. Survival after death is merely an idea. You do not know, but you believe, because belief gives you comfort. You never go into the question of death itself, because the very idea of coming to an end, of entering the totally unknown, is a horror to you that awakens fear. Being afraid, you resort to various forms of belief as a means of escape.

Surely, to free the mind from fear, you have to know what it is to die while you are physically and mentally vigorous, going to the office, attending to everything. You have to know the nature of death while living. Belief is not going to remove fear. You may read any number of books about the hereafter, but that is not going to free the mind from fear, because the mind is used to just one thing, which is continuity through memory, and so the very idea of coming to an end is a horror. The constant recollection of the things you have experienced and enjoyed, everything you have possessed, the character you have built up, your ideals, your visions, your knowledge—all that is coming to an end. And how is the mind to be free of fear? *That* is the problem, not whether there is a continuity after death.

If I am to be free of the fear of ending, surely I must inquire into the nature of death. I must experience it; I must know what it is: its beauty, its tremendous quality. It must be an extraordinary thing to die, to enter into something never imagined, totally unknown.

Now how is the mind to experience, while living, that ending called death? Death is ending. It is the ending of the body and perhaps also of the mind. I am not discussing whether or not there is survival. I am concerned with ending. Can I not end while I am living? Cannot my mind—with all its thoughts, its activities, its memories—come to an end while I am living, while the body is not broken down through old age and disease or swept away by an accident? Cannot the mind, which has built up a continuity, come to an end, not at the last moment but *now*? That is, cannot the mind be free of all the accumulations of memory?

You are a Hindu, a Christian, or what you will. You are shaped by the past, by custom, by tradition. You are greed, envy, joy, pleasure, the appreciation of something beautiful, the agony of not being loved, of not being able to fulfill—you are all that, which is the process of continuity. Take just one form of it. You are attached to your property, to your wife. That is a fact. I am not talking about detachment. You are attached to your opinions, to your ways of thinking.

Now, can you not come to the end of that attachment? Why are you attached? That is the question, not how to be detached. If you try to be detached, you merely cultivate the opposite, and therefore contradiction continues. But the moment your mind is free of attachment, it is also free from the sense of continuity through attachment, is it not? So why are you attached? Because you are afraid that without attachment you will be nothing; therefore you *are* your house, you *are* your wife, you *are* your bank account, you *are* your job. You are all these things. And if there is an ending to this sense of continuity through attachment, a total ending, then you will know what death is.

Do you understand, sirs? I hate, let us say, and I have carried this hatred in my memory for years, constantly battling against it. Can I instantly stop hating? Can I drop it with the finality of death?

When death comes, it does not ask your permission; it comes and takes you; it destroys you on the spot. In the same way, can you totally drop hate, envy, pride of possession, attachment to beliefs, to opinions, to ideas, to a particular way of thinking? Can you drop all that in an instant? There is no "how to drop it," because that is only another form of continuity. To drop opinion, belief, attachment, greed, or envy is to die—to die every day, every moment. If there is the coming to an end of all ambition from moment to moment, then you will know the extraordinary state of being nothing, of coming to the abyss of an eternal movement, as it were, and dropping over the edge, which is death.

I want to know all about death, because death may be reality; it may be what we call "God," that most extraordinary something that lives and moves yet has no beginning and no end. So I want to know all about death. For that I must die to everything I already know. The mind can be aware of the unknown only when it dies to the known—dies without any motive, without the hope of reward or the fear of punishment. Then I can find out what death is while I am living—and in that very discovery there is a freedom from fear. Whether or not there is a continuity after the body dies is irrelevant. Whether or not you are born again is a trivial affair.

To me, living is not apart from dying because in living there is death. There is no separation between death and life. One knows death because the mind is dying every minute, and in that very ending there is renewal, newness, freshness, innocence—not in continuity. But for most of us, death is a thing that the mind has really never experienced. To experience death while living, all the trickeries of the mind—which prevent that direct experiencing—must cease.

I wonder if you have ever known what love is? Because I think death and love walk together. Death, love, and life are one and the same. But we have divided life, as we have divided the earth. We talk of love as being either carnal or spiritual and have set a battle going between the sacred and the profane. We have divided what love *is* from what love *should be*, so we never know what love is. Love, surely, is a total feeling that is not sentimental and in which there is no sense of separation. It is complete purity of feeling without the separative, fragmenting quality of the intellect. Love has no sense of continuity. Where there is a sense of continuity, love is already dead, and it smells of yesterday, with all its ugly memories, quarrels, brutalities. To love, one must die.

Death is love—the two are not separate. But do not be mesmerized by my words. You have to experience this; you have to know it, taste it, discover it for yourself.

The fear of complete loneliness, isolation, of not being anything, is the basis, the very root of our self-contradiction. Because we are afraid to be nothing, we are splintered up by many desires, each desire pulling in a different direction. That is why, if the mind is to know total, non-contradictory action—an action in which going to the office is the same as not going to the office, or the same as becoming a sannyasi, or the same as meditation, or the same as looking at the skies of an evening—there must be freedom from fear. But there can be no freedom from fear unless you experience it, and you cannot experience fear as long as you find ways and means of escaping from it. Your God is a marvelous escape from fear. All your rituals, your books, your theories and beliefs, prevent you from actually experiencing it. You will find that only in ending is there a total cessation of fear—the ending of yesterday, of what has been, which is the soil in which fear sinks its roots. Then you will discover that love and death and living are one and the same. The mind is free only when the accumulations of memory have dropped away. Creation is in ending, not in continuity. Only then is there the total action that is living, loving, and dying.

Life, Death, and Survival

It was a magnificent old tamarind tree, full of fruit, and with tender new leaves. Growing by a deep river, it was well watered, and it gave just the right amount of shade for animals and men. There was always some kind of bustle and noise going on under it, loud talking, or a calf calling for its mother. It was beautifully proportioned, and against the blue sky its shape was splendid. It had ageless vitality. It must have witnessed many things as through countless summers it watched the river and the goings-on along its banks. It was an interesting river, wide and holy, and pilgrims came from all parts of the country to bathe in its sacred waters. There were boats on it, moving silently, with dark, square sails. When the moon rose full and almost red, making a silvery path on the dancing waters, there would be rejoicing in the neighboring village, and in the village across the river. On holy days the villagers came down to the water's edge, singing joyous, lilting songs. Bringing their food, with much chattering and laughter, they would bathe in the river; then they would put a garland at the foot of the great tree and red and yellow ashes around its trunk, for it too was sacred, as all trees are. When at last the chatter and shouting had ceased, and everyone had gone home, a lamp or two would remain burning, left by some pious villager; these lamps consisted of a homemade wick in a little terra cotta saucer of oil, which the villager could ill afford. Then the tree was supreme; all things were of it: the earth, the river, the people, and the stars. Presently it would withdraw into itself, to slumber till touched by the first rays of the morning sun.

Often they would bring a dead body to the edge of the river. Sweeping the ground close to the water, they would first put down heavy logs as a foundation for the pyre and then build it up with lighter wood; on the top they would place the body, covered with a new white cloth. The nearest relative would then put a burning torch to the pyre, and huge flames would leap up in the darkness, lighting the water and the silent faces of the mourners and friends who sat around the fire. The tree would gather some of the light and give its peace to the dancing flames. It took several hours for the body to be consumed, but they would all sit around till there was nothing left except bright embers and little tongues of flame. In the midst of this enormous silence, a baby would suddenly begin to cry, and a new day would have begun.

He had been a fairly well-known man. He lay dying in the small house behind the wall, and the little garden, once cared for, was now neglected. He was surrounded by his wife and children, and by other near relatives. It might be some months, or even longer, before he passed away, but they were all around him, and the room was heavy with grief. As I came in, he asked them all to go away, and they reluctantly left, except a little boy who was playing with some toys on the floor. When they had gone out, he waved me to a chair, and we sat for some time without saying a word, while the noises of the household and the street crowded the room.

He spoke with difficulty. "You know, I have thought a great deal for a number of years about living and even more about dying, for I have had a protracted illness. Death seems such a strange thing. I have read various books dealing with this problem, but they were all rather superficial."

Aren't all conclusions superficial?

"I am not so sure. If one could arrive at certain conclusions that were deeply satisfying, they would have some significance. What's wrong with arriving at conclusions, so long as they are satisfying?"

There's nothing wrong with it, but doesn't it trace a deceptive horizon? The mind has the power to create every form of illusion, and to be caught in it seems so unnecessary and immature.

"I have lived a fairly rich life and have followed what I thought to be my duty, but of course I am human. Anyway, that life is all over now, and here I am a useless thing, but fortunately my mind has not yet been affected. I have read much, and I am still as eager as ever to know what happens after death. Do I continue, or is there nothing left when the body dies?"

Sir, if one may ask, why are you so concerned to know what happens after death?

"Doesn't everyone want to know?"

Probably they do, but if we don't know what living is, can we ever know what death is? Living and dying may be the same thing, and the fact that we have separated them may be the source of great sorrow.

"I am aware of what you have said about all this in your talks, but still I want to know. Won't you please tell me what happens after death? I won't repeat it to anyone."

Why are you struggling so hard to know? Why don't you allow the whole ocean of life and death to be, without poking a finger into it?

"I don't want to die," he said, his hand holding my wrist. "I have always been afraid of death; and though I have tried to console myself with rationalizations and beliefs, they have only acted as a thin veneer over this deep agony of fear. All my reading about death has been an effort to escape from this fear, to find a way out of it, and it is for the same reason that I am begging to know now."

Will any escape free the mind from fear? Does not the very act of escaping breed fear?

"But you can tell me, and what you say will be true. This truth will liberate me…"

We sat silent for a while. Presently he spoke again.

"That silence was more healing than all my anxious questioning. I wish I could remain in it and quietly pass away, but my mind won't let me. My mind has become the hunter as well as the hunted. I am tortured. I have acute physical pain, but it's nothing compared to what's going on in my mind. Is there an identified continuity after death? This 'me,' which has enjoyed, suffered, known—will it continue?"

What is this "me" to which your mind clings and that you want to be continued? Please don't answer, but quietly listen, will you? The "me" exists only through identification with property, with a name, with the family, with failures and successes, with all the things you have been and want to be. You are that with which you have identified yourself; you are made up of all that, and without it you are not. It is this identification with people, property, and ideas that you want to be continued, even beyond death; and is it a living thing? Or is it just a mass of contradictory desires, pursuits, fulfillments, and frustrations with sorrow outweighing joy?

"It may be what you suggest, but it's better than not knowing anything at all."

Better the known than the unknown, is that it? But the known is so small, so petty, so confining. The known is sorrow, and yet you crave for its continuance.

"Think of me, be compassionate, don't be so unyielding. If only I knew, I could die happily."

Sir, don't struggle so hard to know. When all effort to know ceases, then there is something that the mind has not put together. The unknown is greater than the known; the known is but as a barge on the ocean of the unknown. Let all things go and be.

His wife came in just then to give him something to drink, and the child got up and ran out of the room without looking at us. He told his wife to close the door as she went out and not to let the boy come in again.

"I am not worried about my family; their future is cared for. It's with my own future that I am concerned. I know in my heart that what you say is true, but my mind is like a galloping horse without a rider. Will you help me, or am I beyond all help?"

Truth is a strange thing; the more you pursue it, the more it will elude you. You cannot capture it by any means, however subtle and cunning; you cannot hold it in the net of your thought. Do realize this and let everything go. On the journey of life and death, you must walk alone; on this journey there can be no taking of comfort in knowledge, in experience, in memories. The mind must be purged of all things it has gathered in its urge to be secure; its gods and virtues must be given back to the society that bred them. There must be complete, uncontaminated aloneness.

"My days are numbered, my breath is short, and you are asking a very hard thing: that I die without knowing what death is. But I am well instructed. Let be my life, and may there be a blessing upon it."

Bombay

Most of us live in a world of myth, of symbols, of make-believe, which is much more important to us than the world of actuality. Because we do not understand the actual world of everyday living with all its misery and strife, we try to escape from it by creating a world of make-believe, a world of gods, of symbols, of ideas, and of images; and where there is this flight from the actual to the make-believe, there is always contradiction, sorrow. If we would be free of sorrow, surely we must understand the world of make-believe into which we are constantly escaping. The Hindu, the Moslem, the Buddhist, the Christian all have their make-believe worlds of symbols and images, and they are caught in them. To them, the symbol has greater significance and is much more important than the living; it is embedded in the unconscious, and it plays an immense part in the life of all those who belong to one or other of the various cultures, civilizations, or organized religions. So if we would be free of sorrow, I think it is important, first of all, to understand the make-believe world in which we live.

If you walk down the road, you will see the splendor of nature, the extraordinary beauty of the green fields and the open skies, and you will hear the laughter of children. But in spite of all that, there is a sense of sorrow. There is the anguish of a woman bearing a child; there is sorrow in death; there is sorrow when you are looking forward to something, and it does not happen; there is sorrow when a nation runs down, goes to seed; and there is the sorrow of corruption, not only in the collective but also in the individual. There is sorrow in your own house, if you look deeply, the sorrow of not being able to fulfill, the sorrow of your own pettiness or incapacity, and various unconscious sorrows.

There is also laughter in life. Laughter is a lovely thing—to laugh without reason, to have joy in one's heart without cause, to love without seeking anything in return. But such a laughter rarely happens to us. We are burdened with sorrow; our life is a process of misery and strife, a continuous disintegration, and we almost never know what it is to love with our whole being.

One can see this sorrowful process going on in every street, in every house, in every human heart. There are misery, passing joy, and a gradual decay of the mind, and we are always seeking a way out. We want to find a solution, a means or a method by which to resolve this burden of life, and so we never actually look at sorrow. We try to escape through myths, through images, through speculation; we hope to find some way to avoid this weight, to stay ahead of the wave of sorrow.

I think we are familiar with all this. I am not instructing you about sorrow. And it would be absurd if you suddenly tried to feel sorrow as you are listening, or if you tried to be cheerful; it would have no meaning. But if one is at all aware of the narrowness, the shallowness, the pettiness of one's own life, if one observes its incessant quarrels, its failures, the many efforts one has made that have produced nothing but a sense of frustration, then one must inevitably experience this thing called sorrow. At whatever level, however slightly or however deeply, one must know what sorrow is. Sorrow follows us like our shadow, and we do not seem able to resolve it. So I would like, if I may, to talk over with you the ending of sorrow.

Sorrow has an ending, but it does not come about through any system or method. There is no sorrow when there is perception of what is. When you see very clearly what is—whether it be the fact that life has no fulfillment, or the fact that your son, your brother, or your husband is dead; when you know the fact as it actually is, without interpretation, without having an opinion about it, without any ideation, ideals, or judgments, then I think there is the ending of sorrow. But with most of us there is the will of fear, the will of discontent, the will of satisfaction.

Please do not merely listen to what is being said but be aware of yourself; look at your own life as if it were your face reflected in a mirror. In a mirror, you see what *is*—your own face—without distortion. In the same way, do please look at yourself now, without any likes or dislikes, without any acceptance or denial of what you see. Just look at yourself, and you will see that the will of fear is reigning in your life. Where there is will—the will of action, of discontent, the will of fulfillment, of satisfaction—there is always fear. Fear, will, and sorrow go together; they are not separate. Where there is will, there is fear; where there is fear, there is sorrow. By *will* I mean the determination to be something, the determination to achieve, to become, the determination that denies or accepts. Surely, these are the various forms of will, are they not? Because where there is will, there is conflict.

Do look at this and understand not just what I am saying but also the implications of will. Unless we understand the implications of will, we shall not be able to understand sorrow.

Will is the outcome of the contradictions of desire; it is born of the conflicting pulls of "I want" and "I don't want," is it not? The many urges, with their contradictions and reactions, create the will of satisfaction, or of discontent, and in that will there is fear. The will to achieve, to be, to become—this, surely, is the will that engenders sorrow.

What do we mean by sorrow? You see a child with a healthy body and a lovely face, with bright, intelligent eyes and a happy smile. As he grows older, he is put through the machine of so-called education. He is made to conform to a particular pattern of society, and that joy, that spontaneous delight in life, is destroyed. It is sad to see such things happen, is it not? It is sad to lose someone whom you love. It is sad to realize that one has responded to all the challenges of life in a petty, mediocre way. And is it not sad when love ends in a small backwater of this vast river of life? It is also sad when ambition drives you, and you achieve—only to find frustration. It is sad to realize how small the mind is—not someone else's mind but one's own. Though it may acquire a great deal of knowledge, though it may be very clever, cunning, erudite, the mind is still a very shallow, empty thing; and the realization of this fact does bring a sense of sadness, sorrow.

But there is a much more profound sadness than any of these: the sadness that comes with the realization of loneliness, isolation. Though you are among friends, in a crowd, at a party, or talking to your wife or husband, you suddenly become aware of a vast loneliness; there is a sense of complete isolation, which brings sorrow. And there is also the sorrow of ill health.

We know that these various forms of sorrow exist. We may not actually have experienced them all, but if we are observant, aware of life, we know they do exist, and most of us want to escape from them. We do not want to understand sorrow; we do not want to look at it. We do not say, "What is it all about?" All that we are concerned with is to escape from sorrow. It is not unnatural; it is an instinctive movement of desire; but we accept it as inevitable, and so the escapes become far more important than the fact of sorrow. In escaping from sorrow, we get lost in the myth, in the symbol; therefore we never inquire to find out if there is an ending to sorrow.

After all, life does bring problems. Every minute, life poses a challenge, makes a demand; and if one's response is inadequate, that inadequacy of response breeds a sense of frustration. That is why, for most of us, the various forms of escape have become very important. We escape through organized religions and beliefs; we escape through the symbol, the image, whether graven by the mind or by the hand. If I cannot resolve my problems in this life, there is always the next life. If I cannot end sorrow, then let me get lost in amusement; or, being somewhat serious-minded, I turn to books, to the acquisition of knowledge. We also escape through over-eating, through incessant talking, through quarrelling, through becoming very depressed. These are all escapes, and not only do they become extraordinarily important to us, but also we fight over some of them—your religion and my religion, your ideology and my ideology, your ritualism and my anti-ritualism.

Do watch yourself, and please don't be mesmerized by my words. After all, what I am talking about is not some abstract theory; it is your own life as you actually live it from day to day. I am describing it, but don't be satisfied by the description. Be aware of yourself through the description, and you will see how your life is caught up in the various means of escape. That is why it is so important to look at the fact, to consider, to explore, to go deeply into what *is*, because what *is* has no time, no future. What *is* is eternal. What *is* is life; what *is* is death; what *is* is love, in which there is no fulfillment or frustration. These are the facts, the actual realities of existence. But a mind that has been nurtured, conditioned in the various avenues of escape, finds it extraordinarily difficult to look at what *is*; therefore it devotes years to the study of symbols and myths, about which volumes have been written, or it loses itself in ceremonies, or in the practice of method, a system, a discipline.

What is important, surely, is to observe the fact and not cling to opinions or merely discuss the symbol that represents the fact. Do you understand? The symbol is the word. Take death. The word *death* is the symbol used to convey all the implications of the fact—fear, sorrow, the extraordinary sense of loneliness, of emptiness, of littleness and isolation, of deep, abiding frustration. With the word *death* we are all familiar, but very few of us ever see the implications of the fact. We almost never look into the fact of death and understand the extraordinary things that are implied in it. We prefer to escape through the belief in a world hereafter, or we cling to the theory of reincarnation. We have these comforting explanations, a veritable multitude of ideas, of assertions and denials, with all the symbols and myths that go with them. Do watch yourselves. This is a fact.

Where there is fear, there is the will to escape; it is fear that creates the will. Where there is ambition, will is ruthless in its fulfillment. As long as there is discontent—the insatiable thirst for satisfaction that goes on everlastingly, however much you may try to quench it by fulfilling yourself—that discontent breeds its own will. You want satisfaction to continue or to increase, so there is the will to be satisfied. Will in all its different forms inevitably opens the door to frustration, and frustration is sorrow.

So, there is very little laughter in our eyes and on our lips; there is very little quietude in our lives. We seem unable to look at things with tranquility and to find out for ourselves if there is a way of ending sorrow. Our action is the outcome of contradiction, with its constant tension, which only strengthens the self and multiplies our miseries. You see this, don't you?

After all, you are being disturbed. I am disturbing you about your symbols, your myths, your ideals, your pleasures, and you don't like that disturbance. What you want is to escape, so you say, "Tell me how to get rid of sorrow." But the ending of sorrow is not the getting rid of sorrow. You cannot "get rid" of sorrow, anymore than you can acquire love. Love is not something to be cultivated through meditation, through discipline, through the practice of virtue. To cultivate love is to destroy love. In the same way, sorrow is not to be ended by the action of will.

Do please understand this. You cannot get rid of it. Sorrow is something that has to be embraced, lived with, understood; one has to become intimate with sorrow. But you are not intimate with sorrow, are you? You may say, "I know sorrow," but do you? Have you lived with it? Or, having felt sorrow, have you run away from it? Actually, you don't know sorrow. The running away is what you know. You know only the escape from sorrow.

Just as love is not a thing to be cultivated, to be acquired through discipline, so sorrow is not to be ended through any form of escape, through ceremonies or symbols, through the social world of the "do-gooders," through nationalism, or through any of the ugly things that man has invented. Sorrow has to be understood, and understanding is not of time. Understanding comes when there is an explosion, a revolt, a tremendous discontent in everything. But you see, we seek to find an easy way in social work; we get lost in a job, a profession; we go to the temple, worship an image; we cling to a particular system or belief. All these things, surely, are an avoidance, a way of keeping the mind from facing the fact. Simply to look at what *is* is never sorrowful. Sorrow never arises from just perceiving the fact that one is vain. But the moment you want to change your vanity into something else, then the struggle, the anxiety, the mischief begins—which eventually leads to sorrow.

When you love something, you really look at it, do you not? If you love your child, you look at him; you observe the delicate face, the wide-open eyes, the extraordinary sense of innocence. When you love a tree, you look at it with your whole being. But we never look at things in that way. To perceive the significance of death requires a kind of explosion that instantly burns away all the symbols, the myths, the ideals, the comforting beliefs, so that you are able to look at death entirely, totally. But most unfortunately and sadly, you have probably never looked at anything totally. Have you? Have you ever looked at your child totally, with your whole being—that is, without prejudice, without approval or condemnation, without saying or feeling, "He is *my* child"? If you can do this, you will find that it reveals an extraordinary significance and beauty. Then there are not you and the child—which does not mean an artificial identification with the child. When you look at something totally, there is no identification because there is no separation.

In the same way, can one look at death totally?—which is to have no fear. It is fear with its will to escape that has created all these myths, symbols, beliefs. If you can look at it totally, with your whole being, then you will see that death has quite a different meaning because then there is no fear. It is fear that makes us demand to know if there is continuity after death, and fear finds its own response in the belief that there *is* or that there *is not*. But when you can look with completeness at this thing called death, there is no sadness. After all, when my son dies, what is it that I feel? I am at a loss. He has gone away never to return, and I feel a sense of emptiness, loneliness. He was my son, in whom I had invested all my hope of immortality, of perpetuating the "me" and the "mine"; now that this hope of my own continuity has been taken away, I feel utterly desolate. So I really hate death; it is an abomination, a thing to be pushed aside, because it exposes me to myself. And I do push it aside, through belief, through various forms of escape. Therefore fear continues, producing will and engendering sorrow.

So the ending of sorrow does not come about through any action of will. Sorrow can come to an end only when there is a breaking away from everything that the mind has invented for it to escape. You completely let go of all symbols, myths, ideations, beliefs because you really want to see what death is, you really want to understand sorrow; it is a burning urge. Then what happens? You are in a state of intensity; you don't accept or deny, for you are not trying to escape. You are facing the fact.

And when you thus face the fact of death, of sorrow, when you thus face all the things you are confronted with from moment to moment, then you will find that there comes an explosion that is not engendered through gradualness, through the slow movement of time. Then death has quite a different meaning.

Death is the unknown, as sorrow is. You really do not know sorrow; you do not know its depth, its extraordinary vitality. You know the reaction to sorrow but not the action of sorrow. You know the reaction to death but not the action of death, what it implies; you don't know whether it is ugly or beautiful. But to know the nature, the depth, the beauty and loveliness of death and sorrow is the ending of death and sorrow.

You see, our minds function mechanically in the known, and with the known we approach the unknown: death, sorrow. Can there be an explosion, so that the known does not contaminate the mind? You cannot get rid of the known. That would be stupid, silly; it would lead you nowhere. What matters is not to allow the mind to be contaminated by the known. But this non-contamination of the mind by the known does not come about through determination, through any action of will. It comes about when you see the fact as it is, and you can see the fact as it is—the fact of death, of sorrow—only when you give your total attention to it. Total attention is not concentration; it is a state of complete awareness in which there is no exclusion.

So the ending of sorrow lies in facing the totality of sorrow, which is to perceive what sorrow is. That means, really, the letting go of all your myths, your legends, your traditions, and your beliefs—which you cannot do gradually. They must drop away on the instant, now. There is no method by which to let them drop away. It happens when you give your whole attention to something that you want to understand, without any desire to escape.

We know only fragmentarily this extraordinary thing called life; we have never looked at sorrow, except through the screen of escapes; we have never seen the beauty, the immensity of death, and we know it only through fear and sadness. There can be the understanding of life, and of the significance and beauty of death, only when the mind on the instant perceives what *is*.

You know, although we differentiate them, love, death, and sorrow are all the same; because surely, love, death, and sorrow are the unknowable. The moment you know love, you have ceased to love. Love is beyond time; it has no beginning and no end, whereas knowledge has. And when you say, "I know what love is," you don't. You know only a sensation, a stimulus. You know the reaction to love, but that reaction is not love. In the same way, you don't know what death is. You know only the reactions to death, and you will discover the full depth and significance of death only when the reactions have ceased.

Do please listen to this as something that vitally concerns every human being, whether he is on the highest or the lowest rung of society. This is a problem for each one of us, and we must know it as we know hunger, as we know sex, as we may occasionally know a benediction in looking at the treetops or at the open sky. You see, the benediction comes only when the mind is in a state of non-reaction. It is a benediction to know death, because death is the unknown. Without understanding death, you may spend your life searching for the unknown, and you will never find it. It is like love, which you do not know. You do not know what love is; you do not know what truth is. But love is not to be sought; truth is not to be sought. When you *seek* truth, it is a reaction, an escape from the fact. Truth is in what *is*, not in the reaction to what *is*.

7 March 1962

Bombay

I would like to talk about the question of death, as age and maturity, time and negation, which is love. But before I go into that, I think we should be very clear and have deeply understood that fear in any form perverts and breeds illusion, and that sorrow dulls the mind. A dull mind, a mind caught in illusion of any kind, cannot possibly understand the extraordinary question of death. We take shelter in illusion, in fancy, in myth, in various forms of story. And a mind so crippled cannot possibly understand this thing that we call death, nor can a mind understand that has been made dull by sorrow.

The question of fear and sorrow is not a thing which you can philosophize about or put away from you through an escape. It is there as your shadow, and you have to deal with it directly and immediately. We cannot carry it over from day to day, however deep we may consider the sorrow or the fear. Whether it is conscious or unconscious, it has to be understood immediately. Understanding is immediate; understanding does not come through time. It is not a result of continuous searching, seeking, asking, demanding. Either you see it totally, completely in a flash, or you don't see it at all.

I would like to go into this thing called death with which we are all so familiar. We have observed it, we have seen it, but we have never experienced it; it has never been our lot to go through the portals of death. It must be an extraordinary state. I would like to go into it, not sentimentally, not romantically, not with a series of built-up structural beliefs, but actually, as a fact, to comprehend it as I would comprehend that crow cawing on that mango tree—as factually as that. But to understand something factually, you must give your attention; as you listen to that bird in the tree—you don't strain, you listen; you don't say, "It is the crow. What a nuisance it is! I want to listen to somebody," but you are listening to that as well as to what is being said. But when you want to listen only to the speaker and resist the bird and the noise it is making, you will hear neither the bird nor the speaker. And I am afraid that is what most of you are doing when you are listening to a complex and profound problem.

Most of us have not given our minds totally, completely. You have never taken a journey of thought towards its end. You have never played with an idea and seen the whole implication of it and gone beyond it. So it is going to be very difficult if you don't give your attention, if you don't listen easily, pleasantly, with a grace, with a playfulness in which there is no restraint, there is no effort. That is a very difficult thing for most of us to do—to listen—because we are always translating what is being said, and we never *listen* to what is being said.

I want to go into this question of death as a fact, not your death or my death, or somebody's death—somebody whom you like, or somebody whom you don't like—but death as a problem. You know, we are so ridden with images, with symbols; for us symbols have an extraordinary importance, more factual than the reality. When I talk about death, you will instantly think of someone whom you have lost, and that is going to prevent you from looking at the fact. I am going to approach it through diverse ways, different ways—not just what is death and what is after death? Those are utterly immature questions. When you understand the extraordinary thing implied in death, you don't ask that question: What is the hereafter? We have to consider maturity. A mature mind will never ask if there is a life hereafter, if there is a continuity.

We have to understand what mature thinking is, what maturity is, and what age is. Most of us know what age is, because we do grow old, whether we like it or not. Age is not maturity. Maturity has nothing to do with knowledge. Age can contain knowledge but not maturity. But age can continue with all the knowledge, with all the traditions it has acquired. Age is a mechanical process of an organism growing old, being used constantly. A body that is constantly being used in strife, in travail, in sorrow, in fear—an organism that is driven—soon ages, like any machine. But an organism that has aged is not a mature mind. We have to understand the difference between age and maturity.

We are born young, but the generation that has aged soon brings old age to the young. The past generation, which has aged in knowledge, in decrepitude, in ugliness, in sorrow, in fear, imposes that on the young. They are already old in age, and they die. That is the lot of every generation caught in the previous structure of society. And society does not want a new person, a new entity; it wants him to be respectable, it molds him, shapes him, and so destroys the freshness, the innocence of youth. This is what we are doing to all the children around here and in the world. And that child, when it grows to adulthood, is already aged and will never mature.

Maturity is the destruction of society, of the psychological structure of society. Unless you are totally ruthless with yourself, and unless you are completely free from society, you will never be mature. The social structure, the psychological structure of greed, envy, power, position, obeying—if you are not free of all that psychologically, then you will never mature. And you need a mature mind. A mind that is alone in its maturity, a mind that is not being crippled, not being spotted, that has no burden whatsoever—it is only such a mind that is a mature mind.

And you have to understand this: maturity is not a matter of time. If you see very clearly, without any distortion, the psychological structure of the society in which you are being born, brought up, educated, then, the instant you see, you are out of it. Therefore there is maturity on the instant, not in time. You cannot mature gradually; maturity is not like the fruit on the tree. The fruit on the tree needs time, darkness, fresh air, sunlight, rain; and in that process it ripens, ready to fall. But maturity cannot ripen; maturity is on the instant—either you are mature, or you are not mature. That is why it is very important psychologically to see how your mind is caught in the structure of the society in which you are being brought up, the society that has made you respectable, the society that has made you conform, that has driven you in the pattern of its activities.

I think one can see totally, immediately, the poisonous nature of society, as one sees a bottle marked "poison." When you see it that way, you will never touch it; you know it is dangerous. But you don't know that society is a danger, that it is the deadliest thing for a person who is mature. Because maturity is that state of mind that is alone, whereas this psychological social structure never leaves you alone but is always shaping you, consciously or unconsciously. A mature mind is a mind that is completely alone; because it has understood, it is free. And this freedom is on the instant. You cannot work for it, you cannot seek it, you cannot discipline yourself in order to get it; and that is the beauty of freedom. Freedom is not the result of thought; thought is never free, can never be free.

If we understand the nature of maturity, then we can look into time and continuity. For most of us, time is an actual reality. The time by the watch is an actual reality—it takes time to go to your house; it takes time to acquire knowledge; it takes time to learn a technique. But is there any other time, except that time? Is there psychological time? We have built up psychological time, the time covered by the distance, the space, between "me" and what I want to be, between "me" and what I should be, between the past that was the "me." So thought builds psychological time. But is there such time? To find out for yourself, you have to consider continuity.

What do we mean by that word *continuity*? And what is the inward significance of that word, which is so common on our lips? You know, if you think about something, such as the pleasure that you have had, constantly, day after day, every minute, that gives to the past pleasure a continuity. If you think about something that is painful, either in the past or in the future, that gives it continuity. It is very simple. I like something, and I think about it; the thinking about it establishes a relationship between what has been, the thought that thinks about it, and the fact that I would like to have it again. Please, this is a very simple thing if you give your mind to it; it is not a complex thing. If you don't understand what continuity is, you will not understand what I am going to say about death. You have to understand what has been expressed by me, not as a theory or a belief but as an actuality that you see for yourself.

If you think about your wife, about your house, about your children, or about your job all the time, you have established a continuity, have you not? If you have a grudge, a fear, a sense of guilt, and if you think about it off and on, recall, remember, bring it out of the past, you have established a continuity. And our minds function in that continuity; all our thinking is that continuity. Psychologically you are violent, and you think about not being violent, the ideal; so, through your thinking about not being violent, you have established the continuity of being violent. Please, this is important to understand. It is very simple once you see this thing: that thought, thinking about something, gives it continuity, whether it is pleasant or unpleasant, whether it gives you joy or gives you pain, whether it is something past or something that is going to take place tomorrow or next week.

So it is thought that establishes continuity in action—such as going to the office day after day, month after month, for thirty years till your mind is a dead mind. And you equally establish a continuity with your family. You say, "It is my family." You think about it; you try to protect it; you try to build a structure, a psychological protection on it and around yourself. And so the family becomes extraordinarily important, and you are destroyed. The family destroys; it is a deadly thing, because it is a part of the social structure that holds the individual. Having established continuity, psychologically as well as physically, then time becomes very important—time not by the watch but time as a means of arriving, time as a means of psychologically achieving, gaining, succeeding. You can't succeed, you can't gain, unless you think about it, till you give your mind to it. So psychologically, inwardly, the desire for continuity is the way of time, and time breeds fear; and thought as time dreads death.

If you have no time at all inwardly, then death is in an instant; it is not something to be frightened of. That is, if every minute of the day thought does not give continuity to either pleasure or pain, to fulfillment or to lack of fulfillment, to insult, to praise, to everything to which thought gives attention, then there is death every minute. One must die every minute—not theoretically. That is why it is important to understand this machinery of thought. Thought is merely a response, a reflex of the past; it has no validity, as has the tree that you actually see.

To understand the extraordinary significance of death—there is a significance of death into which I shall go presently—you must understand this question of continuity, see the truth of it, see the mechanism of thought that creates continuity.

I like your face; I think about it, and I have established a relationship with you in continuity. I do not like you; I think about it, and I establish it. Now if you don't think about what gives you pleasure or pain, or of tomorrow, or of what you are going to get—whether you are going to succeed, whether you are going to achieve fame, notoriety, and all the rest of it—if you don't think at all about your virtue, about your respectability, about what people say or do not say, if you are totally, completely indifferent, then there is no continuity.

I do not know if you are at all indifferent to anything. I do not mean getting used to things. You have got used to the ugliness of Bombay, the filth of the streets, the way you live. You have got used to it; that does not mean you are indifferent. Getting used to something, as habit, dulls the mind, makes the mind insensitive. But being indifferent is something entirely different. Indifference comes into being when you deny, negate a habit. When you see the ugly and are aware of it, when you see the beautiful sky in the evening and are aware of it, neither wanting nor denying, neither accepting nor pushing it away, never closing the door to anything, and so being completely, inwardly sensitive to everything around you, then out of that comes an indifference that has an extraordinary strength. And what is strong is vulnerable, because there is no resistance. But the mind that only resists is caught in habit, and therefore is a dull, stupid, insensitive mind.

A mind that is indifferent is aware of the shoddiness of our civilization, the shoddiness of our thought, the ugly relationships; it is aware of the street, of the beauty of a tree, or of a lovely face, a smile; and it neither denies it nor accepts it but merely observes— not intellectually, not coldly, but with that warm affectionate indifference. Observation is not detachment, because there is not attachment. It is only when the mind is attached—to your house, to the family, to some job—that you talk about detachment. But, you know, when you are indifferent, there is a sweetness to it, there is a perfume to it, there is a quality of tremendous energy. (This may not be the meaning of that word in the dictionary.) One has to be indifferent—to health, to loneliness, to what people say or do not say, indifferent to whether one succeeds or does not succeed, indifferent to authority.

If you hear somebody shooting, making a lot of noise with a gun, you can very easily get used to it, and you turn a deaf ear; that is not indifference. Indifference comes into being when you listen to that noise with no resistance, go with that noise, ride on that noise infinitely. Then that noise does not affect you, does not pervert you, does not make you indifferent. Then you listen to every noise in the world—the noise of your children, of your wife, of the birds, the noise of the chatter the politicians make—you listen to it completely with indifference and therefore with understanding.

A mind that would understand time and continuity must be indifferent to time and not seek to fill that space that you call time with amusement, with worship, with noise, with reading, with going to the film, with every means that you are using now. And by filling it with thought, with action, with amusement, with excitement, with drink, with woman, with man, with God, with your knowledge, you have given it continuity, and so you will never know what it is to die.

You see, death is destruction. It is final; you can't argue with it. You can't say, "No, wait a few days more." You can't discuss, you can't plead; it is final; it is absolute. We never face anything final, absolute. We always go around it, and that is why we dread death. We can invent ideas, hopes, fears, and have beliefs such as "we are going to be resurrected, be born again"—those are all the cunning ways of the mind, hoping for a continuity, which is of time, which is not a fact, which is merely of thought. You know, when I talk about death, I am not talking about your death or my death— I am talking about *death*, that extraordinary phenomenon.

For you a river means the river with which you are familiar, the Ganges, or the river around your village. Immediately when the word *river* is mentioned, the image of a particular river comes into your mind. But you will never know the real nature of all the rivers, what a real river is, if the symbol of a particular river arises in your mind. The river is the sparkling water, the lovely banks, the trees on the bank—not any particular river, but the riverness of all the rivers, the beauty of all the rivers, the lovely curve of every stream, every flush of water. A man that sees only a particular river has a petty, shallow mind. But the mind that sees the river as a movement, as water—not of any country, not of any time, not of any village, but its beauty—that mind is out of the particular.

If you think of a mountain, being an Indian brought up with all the so-called religious books and all the rest of it, you will probably visualize the Himalayas. Mountain means the Himalayas to you. So you have an image of it immediately, but the mountain is not the Himalayas. The mountain is that height in the blue sky, of no country, covered with whiteness, shaped by the wind, by earthquakes.

When a mind thinks of mountains vastly, or of rivers of no country, then such a mind is not a petty mind; it is not caught by littleness. If you think of a family, you think immediately of *your* family, and so the family becomes a deadly thing. And you can never discuss the whole issue of a family in general, because you are always relating, through continuity of thought, to the particular family to which you belong.

So when we talk about death, we are not talking about your death or my death. It does not really very much matter if you die or I die; we are going to die, happily or in misery—die happily, having lived fully, completely, with every sense, with all our being, fully alive, in full health, or die like miserable people crippled with age, frustrated, in sorrow, never knowing a day, happy, rich, never having a moment in which we have seen the sublime. So I am talking about Death, not about the death of a particular person.

Death is the ending. And what we are frightened about, what we dread, is the ending—the ending of your job, the putting away, the going away, the ending of your family, of the person whom you think you love, the ending of a continuous thing that you have thought about for years. What you dread is the ending. I do not know if you have ever deliberately, consciously, purposely thought of ending something—your smoking, your drinking, your going to the temple, your desire for power—ending it completely, on the instant, as a surgeon's knife cuts cancer. Have you ever tried to cut the thing that is most pleasurable to you? It is easy to cut something that is painful, but it is not easy deliberately to cut with a surgical precision and with compassionate precision something pleasurable, not knowing what is going to happen tomorrow, not knowing what is going to happen in the next instant after you cut. If you cut knowing what is going to happen, then you are not operating. If you have done it, you will know what it means to die.

If you have cut everything around you—every psychological root, hope, despair, guilt, anxiety, success, attachment—then out of this operation, this denial of this whole structure of society, not knowing what will happen to you when you are operating completely, out of this total denial there is the energy to face that which you call death. The very dying to everything that you have known—deliberately cutting away everything that you have known—is dying. You try it some time—not as a conscious, deliberate, virtuous act to find out—just try it, play with it; for you learn more out of play than out of deliberate conscious effort. When you so deny, you have destroyed. And you must destroy, for surely out of destruction purity can come, an unspotted mind.

There is nothing psychological that the past generation has built that is worth keeping. Look at the society, the world that the past generation has brought about. If one tried to make the world more confused, more miserable, one could not do it. You have to wipe all that away instantly, sweep it down the gutter. And to cut it, to sweep it away, to destroy it, you need understanding and also something much more than understanding. A part of that understanding is this compassion.

You see, we do not love. Love comes only when there is nothing, when you have denied the whole world—not an enormous thing called "the world" but just your world, the little world in which you live—the family, the attachment, the quarrels, the domination, your success, your hopes, your guilts, your obediences, your gods, and your myths. When you deny all that world, when there is absolutely nothing left, no gods, no hopes, no despairs, when there is no seeking, then out of that great emptiness comes love, which is an extraordinary reality, which is an extraordinary fact not conjured up by the mind, which has a continuity with the family through sex, through desire.

And if you have no love—which is really the unknown— do what you will, the world will be in chaos. Only when you deny totally the known—what you know, your experiences, your knowledge, not the technological knowledge but the knowledge of your ambitions, your experiences, your family— when you deny the known completely, when you wipe it away, when you die to all that, you will see that there is an extraordinary emptiness, an extraordinary space in the mind. And it is only that space that knows what it is to love. And it is only in that space that there is creation—not the creation of children or putting a painting on canvas, but that creation that is the total energy, the unknowable. But to come to that, you must die to everything that you have known. And in that dying, there is great beauty, there is inexhaustible life energy.

London

I would like to talk about time and death, and I would also like to talk about what we call love.

We are not dealing with ideas. Ideas are organized thought, and thought does not solve our deep psychological problems. What really wipes away our problems is facing them, not through the screen of thought but coming directly and vitally into contact with them, actually seeing and feeling the fact. If I may use the word, one has to be *emotionally*—not sentimentally but emotionally—in contact with the fact. If we rely on thought, however clever, however well organized, however learned, logical, sane, rational it may be, our psychological problems will never be solved. Because it is thought that creates all our problems. One who would really go into this whole question of death and not run away from it must find out for oneself how thought creates time, and how thought also prevents us from understanding the meaning, the significance, and profundity of death.

Most of us are frightened of death, and we try to escape from that fear by rationalizing death or clinging to various beliefs, rational or irrational, again manufactured by thought. To go into this question of death demands, it seems to me, a mind that is not only rational, logical, sane, but that is also able to look directly at the fact, to see death as it is and not be overwhelmed by fear.

To understand fear, we must understand time. I do not mean time by the watch, chronological time. That is fairly simple; that is mechanical; there is nothing much to understand. I am talking about psychological time: the looking back to many yesterdays, to all the things that we have known, felt, enjoyed, gathered, and stored up in memory. Remembrance of the past shapes our present, which in turn is projected into the future. This whole process is psychological time, in which thought is caught. Thought is the result of yesterday passing through today to tomorrow. The thought of the future is conditioned by the present, which again is conditioned by the past.

The past is made up of the things that the conscious mind learned at school, the jobs it has held, the technical knowledge it has acquired, and so on, all of which are part of the mechanical process of remembering; but it is also made up of psychological knowledge, the things that one has experienced and stored away, the memories that are hidden deep in the unconscious. Most of us have not the time to inquire into the unconscious; we are too busy, too occupied with our daily activities; so the unconscious gives various hints and intimations in the form of dreams, and these dreams then require interpretation.

All this, both the conscious and the unconscious processes, is psychological time—time as knowledge, time as experience, time as distance between what *is* and what *should be*, time as a means to arrive, to succeed, to fulfill, to become. The conscious mind is shaped by the unconscious, and it is very difficult to understand the hidden motives, purposes, and compulsions of the unconscious, because we cannot feel our way into the unconscious through conscious effort. It must be approached negatively, not by the positive process of analysis. The analyzer is conditioned by his memories, and his positive approach to something that he does not know and of which he is not fully aware is of very little significance.

Similarly, we must approach death negatively, because we don't know what it is. We have seen others die. We know there is death through disease, old age, and decay, death through accident, and death with a purpose, but we don't really know what it means to die. We may rationalize death. Seeing old age coming upon us—gradual senility, losing our memory, and so on—we may say, "Well, life is a process of birth, growth, and decay, and the ending of the physical mechanism is inevitable." But that doesn't bring deep understanding of what death is.

Death must be something extraordinary, as life is. Life is a total thing. Sorrow, pain, anguish, joy, absurd ideas, possession, envy, love, the aching misery of loneliness—all that is life. And to understand death, we must understand the whole of life, not take just one fragment of it and live with that fragment, as most of us do. In the very understanding of life there is the understanding of death, because the two are not separate.

We are not dealing with ideas or beliefs, because they solve nothing. A man who would know what it means to die, who would actually experience and know the full significance of it, must be aware of death in living; that is, he must die every day. Physically you can't die every day, although there is a physiological change going on every moment. I am talking about dying psychologically, inwardly. The things that we have gathered as experience, as knowledge, the pleasures and pains we have known—dying to all that.

But you see, most of us don't want to die, because we are content with our living. And our living is very ugly; it is mean, envious, a constant strife. Our living is a misery, with occasional flashes of joy that soon become only a memory, and our death is also a misery. But real death is to die psychologically to everything we know—which means being able to face tomorrow without knowing what tomorrow is. This is not a theory or a fanciful belief. Most people are afraid of death and therefore believe in reincarnation, in resurrection, or cling to some other form of belief. But a man who really wants to find out what death is is not concerned with belief. Merely to believe is immature. To find out what death is, you must know how to die psychologically.

I don't know if you have ever tried to die to something that is very close to you and that gives you immense pleasure—to die to it, not with reason, not with conviction or a purpose, but just to die to it as a leaf falls from the tree. If you can die in this way every day, every minute, then you will know the ending of psychological time. And it seems to me that for a mature mind, for a mind that would really inquire, death in this sense is very important. Because to inquire is not to seek with a motive. You cannot find out what is true if you have a motive, or if you are conditioned by a belief, by a dogma. You must die to all that—die to society, to organized religion, to the various forms of security to which the mind clings.

Beliefs and dogmas offer psychological security. We see that the world is in a mess; there is universal confusion, and everything is changing very rapidly. Seeing all this, we want something lasting, enduring, so we cling to a belief, to an ideal, to a dogma, to some form of psychological security; and this prevents us from really finding out what is true.

To discover something new, you must come to it with an innocent mind, a mind that is fresh, young, uncontaminated by society. Society is the psychological structure of envy, greed, ambition, power, prestige; and to find out what is true, one has to die to that whole structure, not theoretically, not abstractly, but actually to die to envy, to the pursuit of "the more." As long as there is the pursuit of "the more" in any form, there can be no comprehension of the enormous implication of death. We all know that sooner or later we shall die physically, that time is passing, and that death will catch up with us; and, being afraid, we invent theories, we put together ideas about death, we rationalize it. But that is not the understanding of death.

You can't argue with physical death; you can't ask death to let you live another day. It is absolutely final. And is it not possible to die to envy in the same way, without argument, without asking what will happen to you tomorrow if you die to envy, or to ambition? This means, really, understanding the whole process of psychological time.

We are always thinking in terms of the future, planning for tomorrow psychologically. I am not talking about practical planning; that is a different matter altogether. But psychologically we want to be something tomorrow. The cunning mind pursues what it has been and what it will be, and our lives are built on that pursuit. We are the result of our memories, memory being psychological time. And is it possible effortlessly, easily, to die to that whole process?

You all want to die to something that is painful, and that is comparatively easy. But I am talking of dying to something that gives you great pleasure, a great sense of inward richness. If you die to the memory of a stimulating experience, to your visions, to your hopes and fulfillments, then you are confronted with an extraordinary sense of loneliness, and you have nothing to rely on. The churches, the books, the teachers, the systems of philosophy—you can't trust any of them any more, which is just as well, because if you put your trust in any of them, then you are still afraid, you are still envious, greedy, ambitious, seeking power.

Unfortunately, when we don't trust anything, we generally become bitter, cynical, superficial, and then we just live from day to day, saying that is enough. But, however cunning or philosophical the mind may be, that makes for a very shallow, petty life.

I do not know if you have ever tried this, if you have ever experimented with it: to die effortlessly to everything that you know, not superficially but actually, without asking what will happen tomorrow. If you can do this, you will come to an extraordinary sense of loneliness, a state of nothingness where there is no tomorrow—and if you go through it, it is not bleak despair. On the contrary!

After all, most of us are terribly lonely. You may have an interesting occupation, you may have a family and plenty of money, you may have the wide knowledge of a learned mind; but if you push all that aside when you are by yourself, you will know this extraordinary sense of loneliness.

But you see, at such a moment we become very frightened. We never face that loneliness; we never go through that emptiness to find out what it is. We turn on the radio, read a book, chatter with friends, go to church, go to the cinema, take a drink—all of which are on the same level, because they all offer an escape. God is a cheerful escape, just as drink is. When the mind is escaping, there is not much difference between God and drink. Sociologically, perhaps, drink is not so good, but the escape to God also has its detriment.

So, to understand death, not verbally or theoretically but actually to experience it, one must die to yesterday, to all one's memories, one's psychological wounds, the flattery, the insults, the pettiness, the envy—one must die to all that, which is to die to oneself. Because all that is oneself. And then you will find, if you have gone so far, that there is an aloneness that is not loneliness. Loneliness and aloneness are two different things. But you cannot come to aloneness without going through and understanding that state of loneliness in which relationship means nothing any more. Your relationship with your wife, with your husband, with your son, your daughter, your friends, your job—none of these relationships has meaning any more when you are completely lonely. I am sure some of you have experienced that state. And when you can go through it and beyond it, when you are no longer frightened by that word *lonely*, when you are dead to all the things that you have known, and society has ceased to influence you, then you will know the other. Society influences you only as long as you belong to it psychologically. Society can have no influence on you whatsoever from the moment you cut the psychological knot that binds you to it. Then you are out of the clutches of social morality and respectability. But to go through that loneliness without escaping, without verbalizing, which is to be with it completely, requires a great deal of energy. You need energy to live with something ugly and not let it corrupt you, just as you need energy to live with something beautiful and not get used to it. That uncontaminated energy is the aloneness to which you must come.

And out of that negation, out of that total emptiness, there is creation.

Surely all creation takes place in emptiness, not when your mind is full. Death has meaning only when you die to all your vanities, your superficialities, to all your innumerable remembrances. Then there is something that is beyond time, something to which you cannot come if you have fear, if you cling to beliefs, if you are caught in sorrow.

New Delhi

To go into the whole problem of death, not theoretically but factually, you need humility. I am using that word *humility* not as a virtue that is cultivated by the vain, by the proud, but as that natural state of mind that comes about when you are really inquiring and really wanting to find out for yourself. Because virtue does not grow within the borders of time. It is a flower that comes into being involuntarily. One hasn't to search for virtue or to cultivate virtue. If you do, it ceases to be virtue. To see the truth that to cultivate virtue is no longer virtue demands a mind that is in a state of humility, because without humility you cannot learn. I am using the word *learn* not in the sense of accumulation, which is knowledge. We are using that word *learning* in the sense of a mind that is not seeking for something, that is not searching for an end with a motive, that is pliable, quick, that is able to see what is true immediately. And to do that you need an extraordinary humility that has in it that peculiar quality of austerity of observation. Austerity, as we know it, is harsh, brutal; it becomes narrow, bigoted, opinionated, dogmatic—but that is not austerity. We are using the word *austerity* in the sense that a mind that has observed, that has seen what is true, is, out of that very observation, in a state of freedom out of which there comes the discipline that is austere.

There must be that austerity with humility, and at that level we are going to commune with each other. You are not going to learn anything from the speaker. If you do, the speaker becomes the authority. Therefore, you cease to be really an observer—a person who is earnestly seeking what is true and putting away what is false; you will become merely a follower, and a follower can never find out what is true. Truth has to be discovered from moment to moment, and you have to discover it—not merely follow the description verbally. You have to find it with all your being, and to find it, you need humility.

One of the things that one observes in the world and within oneself is the peculiar state of mind that is constantly declining, deteriorating. I do not know if you have observed for yourself your own mind, not theoretically, not in terms of a formula or in terms of success and non-success, but with the quality of the mind that can sustain efficiency, clarity, the capacity to observe what is true, without an opinion, without a thought. When one observes not only the minds of others but also one's own mind, one finds that there is a slow decline, not that one has ever reached a height from which one declines; one finds that one does not have the sharpness, the clarity, the energy, the precision required for observation, for a reasoned observation without any sentimentality. Most of us are dull, settled in comforting belief, with a job, a position, a family to maintain, and we live in the darkness of security. When one begins to observe for oneself one's own mind, one must have seen for oneself how the mind, as it grows, as the physical organism matures, gradually begins to decline. We accept this disintegration, this deterioration, and we are not aware. And when we do become aware of it, it becomes a tremendous conflict—how to maintain the mind that is getting worse, that is declining? Probably we have never put to ourselves the question whether the mind need ever decline. Probably we have never found for ourselves by putting that question whether it is possible to stop the deterioration, the decline.

After all, the decline of the mind, the worsening of sensitivity, the coarsening of all our observation—that is truly death, is it not? So, must we not find out for ourselves whether it is possible at all times to sustain a quality of mind that knows no decline? When I use the word *mind*, I include in that the brain—the totality—not just the capacity to acquire a particular technique and to function along that technique for the rest of your life and then die. I am using the word *mind* in the sense not only of the conscious mind but also of the unconscious mind, in which the brain is included—the brain with all its reactions, the brain that thinks, that acts, that gets irritated, that responds to all the nervous strains. We observe, as we grow older, that this thing begins to decline. Observe the old people; observe all the old politicians; observe how even the young people want to fall into the groove of a particular thought and run along that groove.

So it seems to us that it is very important to find out for ourselves whether it is possible to sustain that clarity of observation, actually, not theoretically—actually in the sense of the living present, in the active present. I use that word *present* not in the sense of time as tomorrow or yesterday or now. The active present is always present; it has no tomorrow or yesterday. You should not have the idea that you will have this active, vital energy tomorrow; you have to be aware of the active present with all your capacity, not technological capacity only but with all your aesthetic powers, with your affections, with your sorrows, with your miseries, the frustrations, the ambitions and the failures and the hopeless agony. Is it possible to be aware of all that and to sustain clarity of observation and innocence of inquiry? If this is not possible, whatever action we do has no vital meaning. It becomes mechanical.

Please observe your own minds. You are not listening to the speaker. Don't be caught in the words of the speaker. He is merely describing, and what is described is not the fact. The word is not the thing; the word *tree* is not the fact, which is the tree. If you would observe the tree, the word has little importance.

We are asking a fundamental question, and you have to find out and discover the truth of it. The question is: Can the mind ever not lose its clarity, its capacity to reason—not according to some prejudice, not according to a particular fancy or opinion or knowledge—and sustain itself in a healthy state without any dark, unexplored, rotting corners? Is it possible? To find that out, one has to be aware of the causes of this decline. Now, we are using the word *cause* merely to indicate the source from which the mind is made dull. By discovering the cause, you are not going to free the mind. You may discover the cause of your illness, but you have to do something about it, you have to go to a doctor, you may have to have an operation; you have to act. But most of us think that by merely discovering the cause, we have solved the whole thing. And so the repetition goes on. The repetition is one of the factors of deterioration—the repeating process, the formation of habits and living in those habits. So the discovery of the cause is not going to free the mind from the factor of deterioration.

One of the major factors of deterioration is imitation, psychological imitation—not putting on a shirt or a coat, or going to the office, or learning a particular technique, which you repeat; that is too superficial. It is the habit-forming mechanism of the mind, which, in psychological states, functions in beliefs, in dogmas, in opinions.

If you observe, you will see how your mind functions in habit. It functions in habit because it is essentially afraid not to be secure. So one of the real factors of deterioration is fear, psychological fear, not the natural normal fear of being bitten by a snake and therefore protecting oneself—that is a different matter.

You know, one of our difficulties is that we are always satisfied with the obvious answer, and we always put the obvious questions. Take the problem of simplicity—"to be simple." Our immediate response, which is fairly obvious, platitudinous, and banal, is: you must have only two [changes of clothing] and have only one meal. Then you are supposed to be very very simple. That is not simplicity at all—it verges on exhibitionism and traditional acceptance of what it is to be simple. But simplicity is something entirely different. To be simple means to have a mind that is clear, without conflict, that has no ambition, that is really incorruptible by its own desires. But we are so easily satisfied by the obvious. We say that a man is a saint because he leads a very simple life, has one meal a day, and two suits; and we think we have solved the problem of simplicity. He may be having a hell of a time inside. A man who is in conflict, however saintly he is, is not a simple man, nor is he a religious man.

In trying to find out what the factors of degeneration are, one must not be satisfied with the obvious question and the obvious answers. One must push those aside and go behind, tear down to find the truth of the matter, and that requires energy. And that energy can come only when you are really not concerned with what is going to happen with your particular life when you are simple. To find out the factors of deterioration, you must inquire; you must ask the fundamental question whether a mind can live without habit, not conforming. This means the whole inquiry into authority, not only the authority imposed but also the authority of one's own experiences, knowledge, visions, and all the rest of it. So one begins to see that there is deterioration as long as there is conflict of any kind, at any level, consciously or unconsciously. And most of our lives are a hideous conflict, without any resolution, without any issue—endless conflict.

So the question is whether habit, conflict, and imitation can end, not eventually, not when you die, but now, in the active present. By imitation I mean not the superficial imitation but the psychological, deep-rooted imitation that is called a method, conforming to a discipline, to a pattern—the Hindu pattern, the American pattern, or the Russian pattern, or the Catholic pattern, and so on. That imitation comes only when there is the urge, the search for comfort in security—psychological security. We seek psychological security inwardly, and therefore there is no outward security for any of us. If you think that over, you will see the truth of the matter.

The desire to be secure breeds fear, fear to live and fear to die. Fear is not an abstract thing. It is actually there like your shadow. Every minute of the day it is there—fear of your boss, fear of your wife, fear of your husband, fear of losing. And with that fear we try to live. So we do not know what it is to live. How can a mind that is afraid live? It can build a shelter; it can warm itself; it can isolate itself; it can follow a pattern, a religious illusion, a fiction; it can live in all that, but it is not living. And this fear makes death as something far away. We put fear many years ahead of us, a great distance between that fact and the illusion that fear has created and that we call living. So our life is neither rich nor full—I do not mean full of knowledge, book learning, or reading the latest book and talking about it endlessly. I mean "rich life" in this sense: it understands, it is clear, sharp, awake, alive, full of energy, and efficient in its own observation and discipline; therefore it can see a tree and enjoy the tree, look at the stars, look at the people without envy. Therefore such a life is not a life of ambition, greed, and the worship of success.

Please, sirs, the speaker means exactly what he is talking about. These are not just words to which you listen, and then you go back to your old life again. We are talking about something very, very serious. There must be a new generation, new people, new minds, not the dead old minds with their fears, with their corruption, with their nationalities, with their petty little governments. A new human being must be brought into being to solve this immense problem of living, and nobody is going to create that human being except you and me. And you have to do it—not in some future generation but immediately, which means one has to see the urgency of the thing. You know, when you see the urgency of something that needs to be done immediately, all your capacities, all your energy, all your efficiency, come into being. You do not have to cultivate them; they are there when you feel the urgency of something—like the urgency of being hungry—and then you act.

We do not know what it is to live, nor do we know what it is to die. The thing that you call "living" is a torture with occasional pleasure, which is a sensation—being well fed, having a good meal, sex, driving a good car, or wanting to drive in a good car, or being envious of those who are driving in a good car, and so on. That is our life. Please observe yourself, and you will see what an ugly, brutal thing living has become, without any love, without any beauty, without any care. That is our life, and we are satisfied with that. We put up with it. We do not say, "I am going to break through and find out." We invent all kinds of spurious and phoney reasons.

To live fully, completely, you cannot possibly have an ideal over there, and you live over here. The ideal has no meaning; it is a fiction. What is a fact is your daily travail, daily anxieties, hopes, fears. That is the actual, and to that we become accustomed; with the memory of our tortures, hopes, fears, ambitions, we turn to look at death, which is far away. So what happens? We are frightened of death, and we are frightened of living.

To find out what death is demands a mind that has no fear. I do not know if you have observed the pilots—those who fly extraordinary aircraft that go a thousand miles and more an hour—how they are trained more than all the yogis put together. They have to face death, and therefore their response must be immediate, unconscious. They are trained for years to face death—to survive they must respond immediately to all the instruments, to all the orders. That is one way of not being afraid of death—that is, to train yourself so completely, to be so involuntary that you die at the orders of another for your country and all the rest of that nonsense. Then there is death by suicide: that is, you face life, and life has no meaning; you have to come to the end of things, and you jump off a bridge, or you take pills. Then there is the other way, the so-called religious way: you rationalize death, because you are going to live the same kind of hideous life in the next life—with torture, agony, despair, with lies, with hypocrisy; and you are satisfied by these beliefs because temporarily they give you comfort; they hide your fear.

Now all those ways of dying are very ordinary, unreal, and undependable. We are talking of dying of a different kind, which is to live with death. You understand? To live with death, not to have this time interval between you and the eventual end. The eventual end may be fifty years or a hundred years hence, or the doctors or the scientists may add another fifty years to it, but the inevitable end is always there. We are talking of a voluntary living with death. I am going into that because that is the only way to resolve the whole question of death, not through beliefs, not through ideals, not through the structure of fear and all the rest of the paraphernalia.

For you to find out what death is, there must be no distance between death and you who are living with your troubles; you must understand the significance of death and live with it while you are fairly alert, not completely dead, not quite dead yet. That thing called death is the end of everything that you know. Your body, your mind, your work, your ambitions, the things that you have built up, the things that you want to do, the things that you have not finished, the things that you have been trying to finish—there is an end of all these when death comes. That is the fact—the end. What happens afterward is quite another matter. That is not important, because you will not inquire what happens afterward if there is no fear. Then death becomes something extraordinary—not sadistically, not abnormally, unhealthily—because death then is something unknown, and there is immense beauty in that which is unknown.

These aren't just words.

So to find out the whole significance of death, what it means, to see the immensity of it—not just the stupid, symbolic image of death—this fear of living and dying must completely cease, not only consciously but also deep down. Most of us want to die, wish to die, because our lives are so shallow, so empty. And our life being empty, we try to give significance, meaning to life. We ask, "What is the purpose of living?" Because our own lives are so empty, shallow, worthless, we think we must have an ideal by which to live. It is all nonsense. Fear is the origin of the separation between that fact that you call death and that fact that you call living. What does it mean actually, not theoretically? We are not discussing theoretically; we are not discussing merely to formulate an idea, a concept. We are not; we are talking of facts; and if you reduce a fact merely to a theory, it is your own misfortune. You will live with your own shadow of fear, and your life will end miserably, as it has begun miserably.

So you have to find out how to live with death—not a method. You cannot have a method to live with something you don't know. You cannot have an idea and say, "You tell me the method, and I will practice it, and I will live with death"—that has no meaning. You have to find out what it means to live with something that must be an astonishing thing; actually to see it, actually to feel it; to be aware of this thing called death of which you are so terribly frightened. What does it mean to live with something that you don't know? I don't know if you have ever thought about it at all in that way. Probably you have not. Being frightened of it, all you have done is try to avoid it by not looking at it or by jumping to some hopeful idea. But you really have to ask the fundamental question, which is to find out what death means and to find out if you can live with it as you would live with your wife, with your children, with your job, with your anxiety. You live with all these, don't you? You live with your boredom, your fears. Can you live in the same way with something that you don't know?

To find out what it means to live not only with the thing called life but also with death, which is the unknown, to go into it very deeply, we must die to the things that we know. I am talking about psychological knowledge, not of things like your home, your office; if you don't have them, you won't get your money tomorrow, or you lose your job, or you have no food. We are talking about dying to the things that your mind clings to. You know, we want to die to the things that give us pain; we want to die to the insults, but we cling to the flattery. We want to die to the pain, but we hold on like grim death to the pleasure. Please observe your own mind. Can you die to that pleasure, not eventually but now? Because you do not reason with death, you cannot have a prolonged argument with death. You have to die voluntarily to your pleasure, which does not mean that you become harsh, brutal, ugly, like one of these saints. On the contrary, you become highly sensitive—to beauty, to dirt, to squalor—and being sensitive, you care infinitely.

Is it possible to die to things, to that which you know about yourself? To die—I am taking a very very superficial example—to a habit, to put away a particular habit either of drinking or smoking, having a particular kind of food, or the habit of sex; completely to withdraw from it without an effort, without a struggle, without a conflict, without saying, "I must give it up." Then you will see that you have left behind the knowledge, the experience, the memories of all the things that you have known and learned and lived by. And therefore you are no longer afraid, and your mind is astonishingly clear to observe what this extraordinary phenomenon is of which man has been frightened through millennia, to observe something with which you are confronted, which is of no time, and which in its entirety is the unknown. Only that mind can so observe, which is not afraid and which is therefore free from the known—the known of your anger, of your ambitions, your greeds, your petty little pursuits. All these are the known. You have to die to them, to let them go voluntarily, to drop them easily, without any conflict. And it is possible—this is not a theory. Then the mind is rejuvenated, young, innocent, fresh, and therefore it can live with that thing called death.

Then you will see that life has an entirely different substance. Then life and death are not divided; they are one, because you are dying every minute of the day in order to live. And you must die every day to live; otherwise, you merely carry along the repetition like a recording, repeating, repeating, repeating.

So when you really have the perfume of this thing—not in somebody else's nostrils but in *your* nostrils, in your breath, in your being, not on some rare occasions but every day, waking and sleeping—then you will see for yourself, without somebody telling you, what an extraordinary thing it is to live, with actuality, not with words and symbols, to live with death and therefore to live every minute in a world in which there is not the known, but there is always the freedom from the known. It is only such a mind that can see what is truth, what is beauty, and that which is from the everlasting to the everlasting.

The Wholeness of Life

Then there is the question of dying, which we have carefully put far away from us as something that is going to happen in the future—the future may be fifty years off or tomorrow. We are afraid of coming to an end, coming physically to an end and being separated from the things we have possessed, worked for, experienced—wife, husband, the house, the furniture, the little garden, the books, and the poems we have written or hoped to write. We are afraid to let all that go because we *are* the furniture, we *are* the picture that we possess; when we have the capacity to play the violin, we *are* that violin. Because we have identified ourselves with those things—we are all that and nothing else. Have you ever looked at it that way? You are the house—with the shutters, the bedroom, the furniture that you have very carefully polished for years, which you own—that is what you are. If you remove all that, you are nothing.

And that is what you are afraid of—of being nothing. Isn't it very strange how you spend forty years going to the office, and when you stop doing these things, you have heart trouble and die? You are the office, the files, the manager or the clerk or whatever your position is; you *are* that and nothing else. And you have a lot of ideas about God, goodness, truth, what society should be—that is all. Therein lies sorrow. To realize for yourself that you are that is great sorrow, but the greatest sorrow is that you do not realize it. To see that and find out what it means is to die.

Death is inevitable. All organisms must come to an end. But we are afraid to let the past go. We are the past. We are time, sorrow, and despair, with an occasional perception of beauty, a flowering of goodness, or deep tenderness, as a passing, not an abiding, thing.

And being afraid of death, we say, "Shall I live again?"—which is to continue the battle, the conflict, the misery, owning things, the accumulated experience. The whole of the East believes in reincarnation. That which you are you would like to see reincarnated. But you are all this: this mess, this confusion, this disorder. Also, reincarnation implies that we shall be born to another life; therefore what you do now, today, matters, not how you are going to live when you are born into your next life—if there is such a thing. If you are going to be born again, what matters is how you live today, because today is going to sow the seed of beauty or the seed of sorrow. But those who believe so fervently in reincarnation do not know how to behave; if they were concerned with behavior, then they would not be concerned with tomorrow, for goodness is in the attention of today.

Dying is part of living. You cannot love without dying, dying to everything that is not love, dying to all ideals that are the projection of your own demands, dying to all the past, to the experience, so that you know what love means and therefore what living means. So living, loving, and dying are the same thing, which consists in living wholly, completely, now. Then there is action, which is not contradictory, bringing with it pain and sorrow; there is living, loving, and dying, in which there is action. That action is order. And if one lives that way—and one *must*, not in occasional moments but every day, every minute—then we shall have social order; then there will be the unity of man, and governments will be run by computers, not by politicians with their personal ambitions and conditioning. So to live is to love and to die.

Bombay

There is a creeper—I think, it is called the morning glory—
that has the extraordinary pale blue color that only flowers have,
or a deep purple with a touch of mauve, or a peculiar white. Only
living flowers have those colors. They come, they bloom in the
morning, the trumpet-shaped flowers—and then within a few
hours they die. You must have seen those flowers. In their death
they are almost as beautiful as when they are alive. They bloom
for a few hours and cease to be, and in their death they do not
lose the quality of a flower. And we live for thirty, forty, sixty,
eighty years in great conflict, in misery, in passing pleasures, and
we die rather miserably without delight in our heart, and in death
we are as ugly as in life.

I am going to talk about time, sorrow, and death. We must,
I think, be very clear that we are talking not about ideas but only
about facts. That flower, blooming, full of beauty, delicate, with
delicate fragrance—that is a fact. And the dying of it after a few
hours when the wind comes and the sun rises, and the beauty of
it even in death—that is also a fact. So we are going to deal with
facts and not with ideas.

You can imagine, if you have got imagination, the color
of those flowers. Have a picture, mentally conjure up an image
of that creeper with its delicate colors, the flowers of delicate
colors, the extraordinary beauty of the flowers. But your image,
your idea about the creeper, your feeling about the creeper, is
not the creeper. The creeper with its flowers is a fact. And your

idea about the flowers, though it is a fact, is not actual. You are not actually in contact with the flower through an idea. I think this must be borne in mind: that we are dealing with facts and not with ideas, and that you cannot touch intimately, directly, concretely, come into contact with a fact through an idea. Death cannot be experienced. One cannot come directly into contact with it through an idea. Most of us live with ideas, with formulas, with concepts, with memory; and so we never come into contact with anything. We are mostly in contact with our ideas, but not with the facts.

I am going to talk about time, sorrow, and that strange phenomenon called "death." One can either interpret them as ideas, as conclusions, or come directly into contact with the whole problem of time and the dimension of time. One can come directly into contact with sorrow—that is, that sense of extraordinary grief. And also one can come directly into contact with that thing called "death." Either we come directly into contact with time, sorrow, love, and death, or we treat them as a series of conclusions—the inevitableness of death or the explanations. The explanations, the conclusions, the opinions, the beliefs, the concepts, the symbols have nothing whatsoever to do with the reality—with the reality of time, with the reality of sorrow, with the reality of death and love. If you are going merely to live, or look, or to come or hope to come into contact with the dimension of time, sorrow, or death, through your idea, through your opinion, then what we are going to say will have very little meaning altogether. In fact, you would not be listening at all; you would be merely hearing words; and, being in contact with your own ideas, with your own conclusions, opinions, you would not be in direct contact.

I mean by "contact": I can touch this table, I am directly in contact with the table; but I am not in contact with the table if I have ideas of how I should touch the table. So the idea prevents me from coming directly, intimately, forcefully in contact. If you are not directly in contact with what is being said, then you will continue living a wasteful life. We have this life to live. We are not discussing the future of life—we will come to that presently. We have this life to live. We have lived wastefully, without life itself having any significance. We live in travail, in misery, in conflict, and so on, and we have never been in contact with life itself. And it would be a thousand pities—at least I think so—if you were merely in contact with ideas and not with facts.

We are going to talk about time. I do not know if you have thought at all about this thing called "time"—not abstractly, not as an idea, not as a definition—if you have actually come into contact with time. When you are hungry, you are in contact directly with hunger. But what you should eat, how much you should eat, the pleasure you want to derive from eating, and so on—those are ideas. The fact is one thing, and the idea is another. So to understand this extraordinary question of time, you must be intimately in contact with it—not through ideas, not through conclusions, but intimately, directly, with tremendous intimacy with time. Then you will be able to go into the question of time and see whether the mind can be free from time.

There is obviously the question of time by the watch, chronological time. Obviously, that is necessary. In that is involved the question of memory, planning, design, and so on. We are not discussing that time, the chronological time of every day. We are going to talk about time that is not by the watch. We do not live only by chronological time; we live much more by a time that is not by the watch. For us, time that is not chronological is much more important, has much more significance, than time by the watch. That is, though chronological time has importance, what has much more importance, greater significance, greater validity for most people is psychological time, time as continuity, time as yesterday, a thousand yesterdays and traditions; time not only as the present but also as the future.

So we have time as the past—the past being the memory, the knowledge, the tradition, the experiences, the things remembered—and the present, which is the passage of yesterday to the time of tomorrow, which is shaped, controlled by the past through the present. For us that, not the time by the watch, has tremendous significance. And in that dimension of time we live. We live with the past in conflict with the present, which creates the tomorrow. This is an obvious fact. There is nothing complex about it. So there is time as continuity, and there is time as the future and the past; and the past shapes our thinking, our activity, our outlook, and so conditions the future.

We use time as a means of evolving, as a means of achieving, as a means of gradual changing. We use time because we are indolent, lazy. Because we have not found the way of transforming ourselves immediately, or because we are frightened of immediate change and the consequences of the change, we say, "I will gradually change." Therefore we use time as a means of postponement, time as a means of gradually achieving, and time as a means of change. We need time by the watch to learn a technique; to learn a language we need a few months. But we use time—psychological time, not time by the watch—as a means of changing, and so we introduce the gradual process: "I will gradually achieve; I will become; I am this, and I will become that, through time."

Time is the product of thought. If you did not think about tomorrow or look back in thought to the past, you would be living in the now; there would be neither the future nor the past; you would be completely living for the day, giving to the day your fullest, richest, most complete attention. As we do not know how to live so completely, totally, fully, with such urgency, in today, bringing about complete transformation in today, we have invented the idea of tomorrow: "I will change tomorrow; I will; I must conform tomorrow," and so on. So thought creates psychological time, and thought also brings fear.

Please follow all this. If you do not understand these things now, you won't understand them at the end. They will be just words, and you will be left with ashes.

Most of us have fears: fear of the doctor, fear of disease, fear of not achieving, fear of being left alone, fear of old age, fear of poverty; these are outward fears. Then there are a thousand and one inward fears: the fear of public opinion, of death, of being left completely alone so that you have to face life without a companion, the fear of loneliness, the fear of not reaching what you call "God." Man has a thousand and one fears. And being frightened, he either escapes in a vast network, subtle or crude, or he rationalizes these fears; or he becomes neurotic, because he cannot understand them, he cannot resolve them; or he completely runs away from fear, from various fears, through identification or social activities, reformation, joining a political party, and so on.

Please, I am talking not of ideas but of what actually is taking place in each one of you. So you are not merely reading my words, but, through the words that are being used, you are looking at yourself. You are looking at yourself not through ideas but by coming directly into contact with the fact that you are frightened—which is entirely different from the idea that you are frightened.

Unless you understand the nature of fear and are completely free of it, your gods, your escapes, your doing all kinds of social work, and so on, have no meaning, because you are then a destructive human being, exploiting, and you cannot resolve this fear. A neurotic human being with his innumerable fears, in whatever he does—however good it may be—is always bringing to his action the seed of destruction, the seed of deterioration, because his action is an escape from the fact.

Most of us are frightened, have secret fears; being afraid, we run away from them. The running away from the fact implies that the objects to which you run away become much more important than the fact. You understand? I am frightened; I have escaped from it through drink, through going to the temple, God, and all the rest of it; so God, the temple, the pub become far more important than fear. I protect God, the temple, the pub much more vigorously, because to me they have become extraordinarily important; they are the symbols that give me the assurance that I can escape from fear. The temple, God, nationalism, the political commitment, the formulas that one has, become far more important than the resolution of the fear. So unless you totally resolve fear, you cannot possibly understand what fear is, what love is, or what sorrow is.

A mind that is really religious, a mind that is really socially minded, a mind that is creative, has completely, totally to put away, or understand, or resolve this problem of fear. If you live with fear of any kind, you are wasting your life, because fear brings darkness. I do not know if you have noticed what happens to you when you are frightened of something. All your nerves, your heart, everything becomes tight, hard, frightened. Haven't you noticed it? There is not only physical fear but also psychological fear, which is much more. Physical fear, which is a self-protective response, is natural. When you see a snake, you run away from it, you jump—that is a natural self-protective fear. It is not really fear; it is merely a reaction to live, which is not fear, because you recognize the danger and you move away. We are talking not only of physical fear but much more of the fear that thought has created.

We are going into this question of fear. Unless you follow it step by step, you won't be able to resolve it. We are going to come into contact directly with fear—not what you are frightened about. What you are frightened about is an idea, but fear itself is not an idea. Suppose one is frightened—as most people, the young and old, are—of public opinion, of death. It does not matter what they are frightened of; take your own example. I will take death. I am frightened of death. Fear exists only in relationship to something. Fear does not exist by itself, but only in relation to something. I am frightened of public opinion. I am frightened of death; I am frightened of darkness; I am frightened of losing a job. So fear arises in connection with something.

Let us say that I am frightened of death. I have seen death. I have seen bodies being burned. I have seen a dead leaf falling to the ground. I have seen so many dead things. And I am frightened of dying, coming to an end. Now there is this fear in relation to death, loneliness, a dozen things. How do I look at or come into contact with fear as I come into contact with a table? Am I making myself clear? To come directly into contact with fear—I hope you are doing it, not merely listening—to come directly into contact with that emotion, with that feeling called "fear," the word, the thought, the idea must not come in at all. Right? That is, to come into contact with a person, I must touch his hand, I must hold his hand. But I do not come into contact with that person, though I may hold his hand, if I have ideas about him, if I have prejudices, if I like or dislike. In spite of my holding his hand, the image, the idea, the thought prevents me from coming into contact directly with that person. In the same way, to come directly into contact with your fear—with your particular fear, conscious or unconscious—you must come into contact with it, not through your idea.

So one must first see how the idea interferes with coming into contact. When you understand that the idea interferes with coming into contact, you no longer fight the idea. When you understand the idea—the idea being the opinion, the formula, and so on—you are then directly in contact with your fear, and there is no escape either verbal, or through a conclusion, or through an opinion, or through any other form of escape. When you are in contact with fear, in that sense, then you will find—as you are finding when we are discussing what we are talking about—that fear altogether disappears. And the mind must be free of all fears, not only the secret fears but also the open fears, the fears of which you are conscious. Then only can you look at the thing called sorrow.

You know, man has lived with sorrow for many thousands, millions of years. You have lived with sorrow; you have not resolved it. Either you worship sorrow as a means to enlightenment, or you escape from sorrow. We put sorrow on a pedestal symbolically identified with a person, or rationalize it, or escape from it. But sorrow is there.

I mean by sorrow the loss of someone, the sorrow of failure, the sorrow that comes upon you when you see that you are inefficient, incapable, the sorrow that you find when you have no love in your heart, that you live entirely by your ugly little mind. There is the sorrow of losing someone whom you think you love. We live with this sorrow night and day, never going beyond it, never ending it. Again, a mind burdened with sorrow becomes insensitive, becomes enclosed; it has no affection, it has no sympathy; it may show words of sympathy, but in itself, in its heart it has no sympathy, no affection, no love. And sorrow breeds self-pity. Most of us carry this burden all through life, and we do not seem to be able to end it. And there is the sorrow of time. You understand? We carry this sorrow to the end of our life, not being able to resolve it. There is a much greater sorrow: to live with something that you cannot understand, which is eating your heart and mind, darkening your life. There is also the sorrow of loneliness, being completely alone, lonely, companionless, cut off from all contacts, ultimately leading to a neurotic state and mental illness and psychosomatic diseases.

There is vast sorrow, not only of a human being but also the sorrow of the race. How do you resolve sorrow? You have to resolve it, just as you resolve fear. There is no future—you can invent a future—there is no future for a person who is living with intelligence, who is sensitive, alive, young, fresh, innocent. Therefore you must resolve fear; you must end sorrow.

Again, to end sorrow is to come into contact with that extraordinary feeling without self-pity, without opinion, without formulas, without explanation; just to come directly into contact with it, as one would come into contact with a table. And that is one of the most difficult things for people to do: to put away ideas and to come into direct contact.

Then there is the problem of death—and with the problem of death, the problem of old age. You all know that death is inevitable—inevitable through senility, through old age, through disease, through accident. Though scientists are trying to prolong life by another fifty years or more, death is inevitable. Why they want to prolong this agonizing existence, God only knows! But that is what we want. And to understand death, we must come into contact with death; it demands a mind that is not afraid, that is not thinking in terms of time, that is not living in the dimension of time.

We have put death at the end of life—it is somewhere there, in the distance. And we are trying to put it as far away as possible, as long away as possible. We know there is death. And so we invent the hereafter. We say, "I have lived; I have built a character; I have done things. Will all things end in death? There must be a future." The future, the afterlife, reincarnation—all that is an escape from the fact of today, from the fact of coming into contact with death.

Think of your life. What is it? Actually look at your life, which you want to prolong! What is your life? A constant battle, a constant confusion, an occasional flash of pleasure, boredom, sorrow, fear, agony, despair, jealousy, envy, ambition—that is your life actually, with diseases, with pettiness. And you want to prolong that life after death!

And if you believe in reincarnation—as you are supposed to believe, as your scriptures talk about it—then what matters is what you are now. Because what you are now is going to condition your future. So what you are, what you do, what you think, what you feel, how you live—all this matters infinitely. If you do not even believe in reincarnation, then there is only this life. Then it matters tremendously what you do, what you think, what you feel, whether you exploit or whether you do not exploit, whether you love, whether you have feeling, whether you are sensitive, whether there is beauty. But to live like that, you have to understand death and not put it far away at the end of your life—which is a life of sorrow, a life of fear, a life of despair, a life of uncertainty. So you have to bring death close; that is, you have to die.

Do you know what it is to die? You have seen death enough. You have seen a man being carried to the burning place where he will be destroyed. You have seen death. Most people are frightened of that. Death is as that flower dies, as that creeper dies with all the morning glories. With that beauty, with that delicacy, it dies without regret, without argument; it comes to an end. But we escape from death through time—which is "it is over there." We say, "I have a few more years to live, and I shall be born next life," or, "This is the only life, and therefore let me make the best of it; let me have the greatest fun; let me make it the greatest show." And so we never come into contact with that extraordinary thing called death. Death is to die to everything in the past, to die to your pleasure.

Have you ever tried without argument, without persuasion, without compulsion, without necessity, to die to a pleasure? You are going to die inevitably. But have you tried to die today, easily, happily, to your pleasure, to your remembrances, to your hates, to your ambitions, to your urgency to gather money? All you want of life is money, position, power, and the envy of another. Can you die to them; can you die to the things that you know, easily, without any argument, without any explanation? Please bear in mind that you are not hearing a few words and ideas, but you are actually coming into contact with a pleasure—your sexual pleasure, for example—and dying to it. That is what you are going to do anyhow. You are going to die—that is, die to everything you know, your body, your mind, the things that you have built up. So you say, "Is that all? Is all my life to end in death?" All the things you have done, the service, the books, the knowledge, the experiences, the pleasures, the affection, the family, all end in death. That is facing you. Either you die to them now, or you die inevitably when the time comes. Only an intelligent person who understands the whole process is a religious person.

The person who takes sannyasi's robes, grows a beard, goes to the temple, and runs away from life is not a religious person. The religious person is one who dies every day and is reborn every day. His mind is young, innocent, fresh. To die to your sorrow, die to your pleasure, die to the things that you hold secretly in your heart—do it—thus you will see you will not waste your life. Then you will find something that is incredible that no one has ever perceived. This is not a reward. There is no reward either. You die willingly, or you die inevitably. You have to die naturally, every day, as the flower dies, blooming, rich, full, and then die to that beauty, to that richness, to that love, experience, and knowledge. To die to that every day, you are reborn, so that you have a fresh mind.

You need a fresh mind; otherwise you do not know what love is. If you do not die, your love is merely memory; your love is then caught in envy, jealousy. You have to die every day, to everything you know, to your hatred, to your insults, to flatteries. Die to them; then you will see that time has no meaning. There is no tomorrow then; there is only the *now* that is beyond the yesterday and the today and the tomorrow. And it is only in the *now* that there is love.

A human being who has no love cannot approach truth. Without love, do what you will—do all your sacrifices, your vows of celibacy, your social work, your exploitations—nothing has any value. And you cannot love without dying every day to your memory. For love is not of memory; it is a living thing. A living thing is a movement, and that movement cannot be caged in words, or in thought, or in a mind that is merely self-seeking. Only the mind that has understood time, that has ended sorrow, that has no fear—only such a mind knows what death is. And therefore for such a mind there is life.

Gstaad

Meditation is this attention in which there is an awareness, without choice, of the movement of all things, the cawing of the crows, the electric saw ripping through wood, the trembling of leaves, the noisy stream, a boy calling, the feelings, the motives, the thoughts chasing each other and going deeper, the awareness of total consciousness. And in this attention, time as yesterday pursuing into the space of tomorrow and the twisting and turning of consciousness have become quiet and still. In this stillness there is an immeasurable, not comparable, movement; a movement that has no being, that's the essence of bliss and death and life; a movement that cannot be followed, for it leaves no path, and because it is still, motionless, it is the essence of all motion.

The road went west, curling through rain-soaked meadows, past small villages on the slope of hills, crossing the mountain streams of clear snow waters, past churches with copper steeples; it went on and on into dark, cavernous clouds and rain, with mountains closing in. It began to drizzle, and looking back casually through the back window of the slow-moving car, from where we had come, we saw the sunlit clouds, blue sky, and bright, clear mountains. Without saying a word, instinctively, we stopped the car, backed and turned and went on toward light and mountain. It was impossibly beautiful, and, as the road turned into an open valley, the heart stood still; it was still and as open as the expanding valley; it was completely shattering. We had been through that valley several times; the shapes of the hills were fairly familiar; the meadows and the cottages were recognizable, and the familiar noise of the stream was there. Everything was there except the brain, though it was driving the car. Everything had become so intense, there was death. Not because the brain was quiet, not because of the beauty of the land, or of the light on the clouds or the immovable dignity of the mountains; it was none of these things, though all these things may have added something to it. It was literally death; everything suddenly coming to an end. There was no continuity; the brain was directing the body in driving the car, and that was all. Literally that was all. The car went on for some time and stopped. There was life and death, so closely, intimately, inseparably together, and neither was important. Something shattering had taken place.

There was no deception or imagination; it was much too serious for that kind of silly aberration; it was not something to play about. Death is not a casual affair, and it would not go; there's no argument with it. You can have a lifelong discussion with life, but it is not possible with death. It's so final and absolute. It wasn't the death of the body; that would be a fairly simple and decisive event. Living with death was quite another matter. There was life, and there was death; they were there inexorably united. It wasn't a psychological death; it wasn't a shock that drove out all thought, all feeling; it wasn't a sudden aberration of the brain or a mental illness. It was none of these things, nor was it a curious decision of a brain that was tired or in despair. It wasn't an unconscious wish for death. It was none of these things; these would be immature and so easily connived at. It was something in a different dimension; it was something that defied time-space description.

It was there, the very essence of death. The essence of self is death, but this death was the very essence of life as well. In fact, they were not separate, life and death. This was not some-thing conjured up by the brain for its comfort and ideational security. The very living was the dying, and dying was living. In that car, with all that beauty and color, with that "feeling" of ecstasy, death was part of love, part of everything. Death wasn't a symbol, an idea, a thing that one knew. It was there, in reality, in fact, as intense and demanding as the honk of a car that wanted to pass. As life would never leave nor can be set aside, so death now would never leave or be put aside. It was there with an extraordinary intensity and with a finality.

All night one lived with it; it seemed to have taken possession of the brain and the usual activities; not too many of the brain's movements went on, but there was a casual indifference about them. There was indifference previously, but now it was past and beyond all formulation. Everything had become much more intense, both life and death.

Death was there on waking, without sorrow, but with life. It was a marvelous morning. There was that benediction that was the delight of the mountains and of the trees.

24 August

It was a warm day, and there were plenty of shadows; the rocks shone with a solid brilliance. The dark pines never seemed to move, unlike those aspens, which were ready to tremble at the slightest whisper. There was a strong breeze from the west, sweeping through the valley. The rocks were so alive that they seemed to run after the clouds, and the clouds clung to them, taking the shape and the curve of the rocks; they flowed around them, and it was difficult to separate the rocks from the clouds. And the trees were walking with the clouds. The whole valley seemed to be moving, and the small, narrow paths that went up to the woods and beyond seemed to yield and come alive. And the sparkling meadows were the haunt of shy flowers. But this morning rocks ruled the valley; they were of so many colors that there was only color; these rocks were gentle this morning, and they were of so many shapes and sizes. And they were so indifferent to everything, to the wind, the rains, and the explosions for the needs of man. They had been there, and they were going to be, past all time.

It was a splendid morning, the sun was everywhere, and every leaf was stirring; it was a good morning for the drive, not long but enough to see the beauty of the land. It was a morning that was made new by death, not the death of decay, disease, or accident but the death that destroys for creation to be. There is no creation if death does not sweep away all the things that the brain has put together to safeguard the self-centered existence. Death, previously, was a new form of continuity; death was associated with continuity. With death came a new existence, a new experience, a new breath, a new life. The old ceased, and the new was born, and the new then gave place to yet another new. Death was the means to the new state, new invention, to a new way of life, to a new thought. It was a frightening change, but that very change brought a fresh hope.

But now death did not bring anything new, a new horizon, a new breath. It is death, absolute and final. And then there's nothing, neither past nor future. Nothing. There's no giving birth to anything. But there's no despair, no seeking; there is complete death without time, looking out of great depths that are not there. Death is there without the old or the new. It is death without smile and tear. It is not a mask covering up, hiding some reality. The reality is death, and there's no need for cover. Death has wiped away everything and left nothing. This nothing is the dance of the leaf; it is the call of that child. It is nothing, and there must be nothing. What continues is decay, the machine, the habit, the ambition. There is corruption, but not in death. Death is total nothingness. It must be there, for out of that life is, love is. For in this nothingness creation is. Without absolute death, there's no creation.

31 August

Meditation without a set formula, without a cause and reason, without end and purpose is an incredible phenomenon. It is not only a great explosion that purifies but it is also death, which has no tomorrow. Its purity devastates, leaving no hidden corner where thought can lurk in its own dark shadows. Its purity is vulnerable; it is not a virtue brought into being through resistance. It is pure because it has no resistance, like love. There is no tomorrow in meditation, no argument with death. The death of yesterday and of tomorrow does not leave the petty present of time—and time is always petty—but a destruction that is the new. Meditation is this, not the silly calculations of the brain in search of security. Meditation is destruction to security, and there is great beauty in meditation, not the beauty of the things that have been put together by man or by nature but of silence. This silence is emptiness in which and from which all things flow and have their being. It is unknowable. Neither intellect nor feeling can make their way to it; there is no way to it, and a method to it is the invention of a greedy brain. All the ways and means of the calculating self must be destroyed wholly; all going forward or backward, the way of time, must come to an end, without tomorrow. Meditation is destruction; it's a danger to those who wish to lead a superficial life and a life of fancy and myth.

The stars were very bright, brilliant so early in the morning. Dawn was far away. It was surprisingly quiet; even the boisterous stream was quiet, and the hills were silent. A whole hour passed in that state when the brain was not asleep but awake, sensitive and only watching; during that state the totality of the mind can go beyond itself, without directions, for there is no director. Meditation is a storm, destroying and cleansing. Then, far away, came dawn. In the east there was spreading light, so young and pale, so quiet and timid; it came past those distant hills, and it touched the towering mountains and the peaks. In groups and singly, the trees stood still; the aspen began to wake up, and the stream shouted with joy. That white wall of a farmhouse, facing west, became very white. Slowly, peacefully, almost begging it came and filled the land. Then the snow peaks began to glow bright rose, and the noises of the early morning began. Three crows flew across the sky, silently, all in the same direction; from afar came the sound of a bell on a cow, and still there was quiet. Then a car was coming up the hill, and a day began.

On that path in the wood, a yellow leaf fell; for some of the trees autumn was here. It was a single leaf, with not a blemish on it, unspotted, clean. It was the yellow of autumn; it was still lovely in its death; no disease had touched it. It was still the fullness of spring and summer, and still all the leaves of that tree were green. It was death in glory. Death was there, not in the yellow leaf but actually there, not an inevitable traditionalized death but that death that is always there. It was not a fancy but a reality that could not be covered up. It is always there around every bend of a road, in every house, with every god. It was there with all its strength and beauty.

You can't avoid death. You may forget it; you may rationalize it or believe that you will be reborn or resurrected. Do what you will, go to any temple or book, it is always there, in festival and in health. You must live with it to know it; you can't know it if you are frightened of it; fear only darkens it. To know it you must love it. To live with it you must love it. The knowledge of it isn't the ending of it. It's the end of knowledge but not of death. To love it is not to be familiar with it; you can't be familiar with destruction. You can't love something you don't know, but you don't know anything, not even your wife or your boss, let alone a total stranger. But yet you must love it, the stranger, the unknown. You only love that of which you are certain, that which gives comfort, security. You do not love the uncertain, the unknown; you may love danger, give your life for another, or kill another for your country, but this is not love; these have their own reward and profit; gain and success you love though there's pain in them. There's no profit in knowing death, but strangely death and love always go together; they never separate. You can't love without death; you can't embrace without death being there. Where love is, there is also death; they are inseparable.

But do we know what love is? You know sensation, emotion, desire, feeling, and the mechanism of thought, but none of these is love. You love your husband, your children; you hate war but you practice war. Your love knows hate, envy, ambition, fear; the smoke of these is not love. Power and prestige you love, but power and prestige are evil, corrupting. Do we know what love is? Never knowing it is the wonder of it, the beauty of it. Never knowing, which does not mean remaining in doubt, nor does it mean despair; it's the death of yesterday and so the complete uncertainty of tomorrow. Love has no continuity, nor has death. Only memory and the picture in the frame have continuity, but these are mechanical, and even machines wear out, yielding place to new pictures, new memories. What has continuity is ever decaying, and what decays isn't death. Love and death are inseparable, and where they are, there's always destruction.

Saanen

You see, I have talked about death so that you might really understand this whole thing—not just now but throughout the rest of your life—and thereby be free of sorrow, free of fear, and actually know what it means to die. If now, and in the days to come, your mind is not completely aware, innocent, deeply attentive, then listening to words is utterly futile. But if you are aware, deeply attentive, conscious of your own thoughts and feelings, if you are not interpreting what the speaker is saying but are actually observing yourself as he describes and goes into the problem, then you will live—live not only with exultation but also with death and with love.

Sources and Acknowledgments

From the Authentic Report of the eighth public talk at Saanen 28 July 1964 in *Collected Works of J. Krishnamurti* copyright © 1992 Krishnamurti Foundation of America.

From the unpublished report of a discussion at Ojai 7 June 1932 copyright © 1992 Krishnamurti Foundation of America.

From the unpublished revision by Krishnamurti of a question asked after the ninth public talk in Bombay 14 March 1948 copyright © 1992 Krishnamurti Foundation of America.

From the Verbatim Report of the second talk at Benares Hindu University Varanasi 17 January 1954 in *Collected Works of J. Krishnamurti* copyright © 1991 Krishnamurti Foundation of America.

From the Verbatim Report of the fifteenth talk with students at Rajghat 22 January 1954 in *Collected Works of J. Krishnamurti* copyright © 1991 Krishnamurti Foundation of America.

From chapter 14 of *Commentaries on Living Second Series* copyright © 1958 Krishnamurti Writings, Inc.

From the unpublished report of a discussion in Seattle 3 August 1950 copyright © 1992 Krishnamurti Foundation of America.

From chapter 2 of *Talks in Europe 1968* 28 April 1968 in Paris copyright © 1969 The Krishnamurti Foundation London.

From chapter 3 of *Talks in Europe 1968* 19 May 1968 in Amsterdam copyright © 1969 The Krishnamurti Foundation London.

From chapter 1 of *The Flight of the Eagle* 20 March 1969 in London copyright © 1971 The Krishnamurti Foundation London.

From the transcript of the sixth public talk at Saanen 17 July 1972 copyright © 1992 Krishnamurti Foundation Trust, Ltd.

From the Verbatim Report of the seventh public talk at Saanen 21 July 1963 in *Collected Works of J. Krishnamurti* copyright © 1992 Krishnamurti Foundation of America.

From the transcript of the third public talk at Brockwood Park 7 September 1974 copyright © 1992 Krishnamurti Foundation Trust, Ltd.

From the transcript of the third public dialogue at Saanen 30 July 1976 copyright © 1992 Krishnamurti Foundation Trust, Ltd.

APPENDIX

Schools, study centers, and foundations in England, India, and the United States that were operated during Krishnamurti's life still seek to apply his approach to education and life—even after his death.

ENGLAND
Information on Brockwood Park School, the Study Center, and the Foundation may be obtained by contacting Krishnamurti Foundation Trust.

Krishnamurti Foundation Trust
Brockwood Park
Bramdean, Hampshire
SO24 0LQ England
Phone: 44 1962 771 525
Fax: 44 1962 771 159
E-mail: info@brockwood.org.uk
www.kfoundation.org

INDIA
For information on the various residential and day schools, study centers, and the Foundation, please contact Krishnamurti Foundation India.

Krishnamurti Foundation India
124/126 Greenways Road
Chennai 600 028
India
Tel: 91 44 2493 7803/7596
E-mail: kfihq@md2.vsnl.net.in
www.kfionline.org

UNITED STATES
For information on Oak Grove School, the Retreat Center, and the Foundation, please contact Krishnamurti Foundation of America.

Krishnamurti Foundation of America
P.O. Box 1560
Ojai, CA 93024-1560
Phone: 1 805 646 2726
Fax: 1 805 646 6674
E-mail: kfa@kfa.org
www.kfa.org